THE MOST INCREDIBLE BASEBALL STORIES EVER TOLD

INSPIRATIONAL AND UNFORGETTABLE TALES FROM THE GREAT SPORT OF BASEBALL

Hank Patton

TABLE OF CONTENTS

ATTENTION:

DO YOU WANT MY FUTURE BOOKS AT HEAVY DISCOUNTS AND EVEN FOR FREE?

HEAD OVER TO <u>WWW.SECRETREADS.COM</u>
AND JOIN MY SECRET BOOK CLUB!

INTRODUCTION

Turn to any page in the baseball history books and you'll find an incredible story. A player who overcame all the odds to become one of the greatest ever players. A team that came back to win it all. A story about perseverance in the face of relentless challenge. These stories explain why baseball is America's favorite pastime. Baseball is a constant source of inspiration that helps drive the nation's spirit.

In these pages, you'll discover some of baseball's most remarkable and inspiring stories and players. Chances are, you already know many of the players and events in this book, but you may not know the *whole* story.

Everyone knows about Babe Ruth, the Great Bambino, but did you know about his difficult childhood? Did you know Ted Williams almost perished in a crash landing during the Korean War? It's these stories that deserve to be told. They help us appreciate how legendary these players truly were in their times.

Learning about these inspirational baseball stories provides insights and lessons you can use in your own life. You don't have to be working towards a baseball career to learn from these players and events. The hard work, grit, and dedication displayed in these stories should inspire you to push for your goals, no matter how distant they feel!

As you're reading, consider the skills and qualities these players exhibit. If you can impart them into your daily routines, you'll crush any pitch that life throws at you.

CHAPTER 1:

LEROY "SATCHEL" PAIGE, A MAN AND A MYTH

Baseball has plenty of mythology throughout its history. Almost every player or team has some drop of folklore that fans love to debate and discuss. Did Babe Rube point to the outfield to call his home run? Was a goat responsible for a curse that kept the Chicago Cubs from winning a World Series for over a century? Did Wade Boggs really drink copious amounts of beer on cross-country flights?

Arguably, no player in history has more of these fact-or-fiction stories than Leroy "Satchel" Paige. Even his age is a story of legend. For years, he changed his birth year in interviews, leading to reporters having differing accounts of his age. Paige claimed he was never sure how old he was, even telling some people that a goat ate his birth certificate. So, his birth year ranged from 1900 to 1908. It's up for debate if any of this was true or if Satchel Paige was just adding to his mystique. His actual birthdate, July 7, 1906, was determined in 1948 when Cleveland Indians owner Bill Veeck traveled to Mobile, Alabama, and accompanied Paige's family to the County Health Department to obtain his birth certificate

Satchel Paige even has an origin story for his pitching prowess, which is not something many baseball players can say. Paige loved baseball from an early age but never had any formal training. Growing up poor in Mobile, Alabama, Paige and his friends would play a baseball-like game using sticks and bottle caps instead of bats and balls.

He wouldn't get a chance to play in any kind of organized format until he was around 12 or 13. Paige found himself in the Alabama Reform School for Juvenile Negro Law-Breakers. The young Paige loved skipping school and shoplifting with friends, eventually getting arrested. It was at the reform school that he would meet Reverend Moses Davis.

Reverend Davis recognized Paige's natural baseball talent. The teenager's tall, skinny frame and strong arm were ideal for pitching. Under the reverend's tutelage, Paige learned the high leg kick and catapult-like delivery that became staples of his career. In his own words, he "traded five years of freedom to learn how to pitch." It didn't take long after his release from reform school at age 18 for Paige to receive his first baseball contract.

Timeless Barnstorming

Satchel Paige's playing career is the definition of barnstorming. Throw a dart at the United States and Central America and you're likely to hit a town or country where Paige took the mound during his career. Barnstorming was the life of many Negro League stars, but few took it to the level of Satchel Paige.

By his own count, Paige started approximately 2,500 games. That is over three times Cy Young's MLB record of

815. While most likely an exaggeration, finding another player who pitched with such obsession-like passion as Paige is impossible. He also claims he played for over 250 teams in his career. This could be another exaggerated unlikelihood but is at least plausible when you look at Paige's track record.

He started playing in Chattanooga and Birmingham before playing in Cuba. He didn't spend long on the island, and there are multiple accounts of why he left abruptly (most end with him being chased off the island by police). Paige then rented his talents to multiple teams, playing in Baltimore, Birmingham, Chicago, Houston, Cleveland, and more.

By the early 1930s, Satchel Paige had solidified himself as one of the Negro League's brightest stars and a deadly pitcher. After playing in Pittsburgh, he joined the California Winter League, an off-season program for top talent from both Black and White baseball. It was here that players like Babe Ruth, Dizzy Dean, and Joe DiMaggio faced Paige for the first time.

Satchel would continue barnstorming for several more years, well into the 1940s. His playing took him all over the US, to Puerto Rico, Mexico, Dominican Republic, back to the US, and so on.

In 1948, his barnstorming days came to a pause when he received a contract to play for the Cleveland Indians in

Major League Baseball. He pitched well and was in the conversation for Rookie of the Year (despite being a veteran of over two decades). He'd later play for the St. Louis Browns, making the 1953 All-Star squad.

Paige would leave the majors and go back to barnstorming, continuing to play all over for many years. He'd come back to Major League Baseball at the age of 59 for a one-game outing for the Kansas City Athletics against the Boston Red Sox. Everyone viewed the event as a publicity stunt and a tip-of-the-hat to Paige's career.

The veteran pitcher had other ideas. Despite having not pitched in the major leagues in over a decade (and nearing 60 years of age), Paige was still dominant. He threw three shutout innings. The only hit off the timeless Paige was a double by Carl Yastrzemski. Diego Segui, who relieved Paige in the fourth inning, said later about the game, "I never expected to see what I saw that day. You don't think a guy that age, he's got all this gray hair, and he's getting everybody out? You don't expect that."

Paige was still pitching in professional games the following year.

Fastballing Folklore

Satchel Paige's career continues to dazzle baseball fans and historians because it is heavily steeped in folklore. This was true of many stars and barnstormers in the Negro Leagues. Not every park accurately tracked player stats or game scores. Sometimes there was no record at all. What did survive from these games are stories. And no player has more stories, told and untold, than Paige.

Part of this was his own design. Paige was as much a showman as he was an incredible pitcher. He reveled in creating drama and humor during games and loved adding to his own mythos (such as changing his age in interviews to confuse reports).

There's no sense in trying to separate fact from fiction. After all, it would only tarnish the mystique behind the man. Instead, consider the following retellings of famous Satchel Paige stories as just that. You can decide for yourself what's real or too incredible to be believed.

The name "Satchel"

For a man whose legend is as well-crafted as a storybook character, it only makes sense to have a story behind the name, too. The L&N Railway Station in Mobile provided lots of Black youths with income, whether it was shining shoes or carrying luggage for White travelers. Satchel's profession was the latter. In his memoir, he says he created a contraption using a pole and rope to help him carry more luggage, which meant more dough in Paige's pocket.

His family members offer a different explanation, saying his feet were the size of a suitcase. Thus, they came to call him "Satchelfoot." Another possible source for the nickname was the boy's penchant for stealing bags, rather than carrying them for passengers.

In either case, once he received the name, he was rarely called Leroy again. Satchel Paige was born.

Satchel Paige's "secret stuff"

There's no debating that Satchel Paige pitched longer and possibly more than any player in history. His three-inning spectacle in 1965 at age 59 makes him the oldest player in Major League Baseball history. That's the reality. The myth is *how* he managed such supreme longevity.

Paige claimed it was thanks to Native American medicine. While playing in North Dakota in 1935, he became friends with members of the Sioux Nation. A medicine man in the tribe gifted him an ointment for his overworked arm. It was reportedly a mixture of rattlesnake venom, gunpowder, and other materials.

While teammates would sometimes remark on the odorous ointment, Paige swore by it. He was known to treat his arm with the oil after every game, claiming it kept his arm "nice and young."

Sitting his fielders

During one game, the fielders behind Satchel Paige made a series of errors that loaded the bases. Paige, working with just a one-run lead, was furious about the mistakes. He demanded his teammates leave the field. With no fielders remaining, any ball hit into play would undoubtedly score the winning runs for the opposing team. Paige then proceeded to strike out the next three batters.

Other accounts claim Paige did this on more than one occasion, as a way of showboating. It didn't always work in his favor.

Facing Josh Gibson in the 1942 Negro League World Series

While Satchel Paige was the most prominent Negro League pitcher, Josh Gibson was the most famous batter. He was the Babe Ruth of Black baseball. Although, Gibson preferred to say that Ruth was the White Josh Gibson.

Years before the 1942 Negro League World Series, the pair were barnstorming in Puerto Rico. Gibson boasted to Paige that the two would meet in a big game, with the bases loaded, and he'd take the pitcher deep.

The Negro League World Series seemed like the perfect example of the "big game" that Gibson had mentioned. Paige claims that after giving up a single, he intentionally walked the next two batters, loading the bases for Gibson.

"Remember Puerto Rico?" Paige says he called out to the slugger at the plate. "Well, the bases is filled. Now you're too smart to fool, so I'm goin' to tell you what's coming." He relayed each pitch he was about to throw and still struck out the formidable hitter.

This is Paige's version (and it changes over different retellings). Whatever really happened between the two Negro League all-stars, the matchup became an instant classic. Satchel's penchant for showmanship and trash-talking made the event even more thrilling for fans and history books.

The gum wrapper and the nail act

Paige's success on the mound was one-part arm strength to fuel his high-velocity pitching, one-part trickery and deception to throw off the hitter's timing, and one-part deadly accuracy to pinpoint the ball exactly where he wanted it.

To hone his accuracy, teammates say he would place a gum wrapper on home plate. The wrapper became his new strike zone. Pitch after pitch, he'd throw the ball right over the wrapper. Another tactic was to stand three bats up at home plate next to one another. The object was to hit the middle one without disturbing the other two. Paige could repeat the feat at will.

Perhaps the most miraculous showcase of his talents was what became known as the nail act. Someone would put nails into a plank of wood, just deep enough that they'd hold. Then, Satchel would take the mound and fire balls into the nail head, driving the spikes into the wood with the proficiency of a hammer. It took both accuracy and power.

With such small targets for practice, the home plate must have been the size of a billboard in Paige's eyes.

Losing his divorce papers

Satchel Paige married Janet Howard in 1934. She quickly became unhappy in the marriage and filed for divorce in 1943. Paige received the news on "Paige Day" at Wrigley Field. He had pitched wonderfully at the event - five hitless innings - and the fans showered him with gifts and autograph requests (not to mention a share of the stadium box-office pot; it was, after all, Satchel Paige Day).

So, when two individuals put a paper in front of him, he assumed it was another fan. The men gruffly informed him that they were *not* interested in an autograph. Instead, they were serving him divorce papers. "You just don't expect to have everything going your way like they do on a special day and then have it cut right off by a divorce summons," Satchel recalled years later.

He took the papers and continued to sign autographs. When no fans were left to meet and greet, he realized he was missing the divorce papers. "I guess somewhere today there's some guy with my autograph on my divorce summons."

Satchel Paige by the Numbers (*)

The stories justify Paige's unrelenting legacy that numbers can't. Almost any other athletic career is defined by statistics, especially in baseball. People talk about the season Ted Williams hit .406 before discussing his impressive military career. It always starts with the statistics. How many strikeouts? How well did he hit? How many World Series titles? It's these stats that offer the necessary fodder for debates on who is the better player and why.

Satchel Paige and other stars from the Negro Leagues don't have meticulous statistics behind their names. There wasn't the money in Black baseball to keep records or report on every game. Paige did keep his own book detailing his pitching appearances. Here are some of Paige's stats, as kept by the man himself:

- 2,500 games pitched
- 2,000 wins
- 250 teams
- 250 shutouts
- 153 pitching appearances in a year

- 62 consecutive scoreless innings
- 50 no-hitters
- 29 starts in a single month
- 22 strikeouts in a game
- 21 consecutive wins
- Three wins on the same day

Most of these numbers are all-time records, if they are true. Again, this is Satchel Paige. Everything has an asterisk or another version. The other thing to consider is that Paige's record-keeping isn't limited to only professional games. Thus, some of his numbers (like pitching 2,500 games) are not as impossible as they first appear.

Even 50 no-hitters (the MLB record is seven by Nolan Ryan) isn't too crazy considering the wide range of talent Paige faced. Bonafide records say he completed the feat against high-level Negro League teams. So, it isn't inconceivable for him to repeat the achievement several times against lesser teams.

There's *some* justification for every one of these records (after all, he pitched until he was almost 60!), but that's the story of Satchel Paige. Everything is plausible and unbelievable at the same time. It's exactly how Paige sculpted his own legend. It's how he intended to be remembered.

Did You Know?

- Despite Jackie Robinson's unbelievable achievements, Paige was actually the first Black player in the Hall of Fame.

- Baseball fans can catch a glimpse of Satchel Paige in the movie *The Wonderful Country*, a 1959 western film starring Robert Mitchum.

- Jackie Robinson broke baseball's color barrier, but Satchel Paige was largely responsible for opening the door. He helped arrange games between Black and White baseball players. He also got stadium owners to allow Negro Leagues to play games at their parks during barnstorming tours. When Robinson was selected to become the first Black player in organized baseball, Paige was angered, feeling that the honors should have been his. He later rescinded these feelings, noting that Jackie Robinson was the right man for the job.

- A famous part of Paige's showboating was his hesitation pitch, where he would pause for a moment in the middle of his windup to unnerve the hitter. He alleged that he learned the hesitation pitch from throwing rocks during fights in his youth. Pausing before releasing the projectile ensured the target didn't dodge the stone. Paige would also go through his windup two or three times to achieve the same effect and disrupt the batter's timing.

- Another element of Paige's theatrics was his love of naming each one of his pitches. There was the "Bat dodger," the "Whipsy-Dipsy-Do," and the "Bee-Ball." He also could throw a "Long Tom," "Wobbly Ball," and "Midnight Creeper."

- Satchel Paige was the seventh Black player to join Major League Baseball and the first Black pitcher in the American League.

CHAPTER 2:

JACKIE ROBINSON AND THE MEANING OF 42

In 1903, a 21-year-old Branch Rickey was coaching the Ohio Wesleyan baseball team. He witnessed his catcher, Charles Thomas, face repeated discrimination because of his skin color. One night, the team arrived at their hotel, but the clerk refused to grant Thomas a room. Rickey bargained to have Thomas stay in his room on a cot. When the coach arrived in the room, he found his catcher distraught and staring at his black skin. "It's my skin, Mr. Rickey. If it weren't for my skin, I wouldn't be any different from anyone; if only my hands were white."

The vision of Thomas in that hotel room would haunt Rickey for years. He decided that, if he ever had the chance, he'd do something about the unfair separation of Blacks and Whites in baseball. Rickey's faith motivated him further, "I cannot face my God much longer knowing that his black creatures are held separate and distinct from his white creatures in the game that has given me all that I call my own," he declared.

As the general manager of the Brooklyn Dodgers, Rickey told some of his closest allies his plan. He was going to bring a Black player to organized baseball, ending baseball's unspoken color barrier that prevented non-Whites from entering the league. Rickey's "Great Experiment," as he'd call it, was about to begin. There was only one piece missing: the Black player capable of seeing the mission through.

The Perfect Candidate

Branch Rickey and his scouting team searched the Negro Leagues for the perfect baseball player to introduce to the Dodgers. Rickey had a list of criteria. The player would have to be good enough to excel against the best major leaguers. He also needed to have experience playing with White teammates. But most importantly, he needed to have the mental fortitude and resilience to ignore the onslaught of bigotry and hate he would face.

Rickey and his team landed on Jack (Jackie) Roosevelt Robinson. The Dodgers sent Clyde Sukeforth to check on his playing performance. Shortly after Sukeforth put his stamp of approval on Robinson's baseball skills, the player was in Rickey's office. The first meeting ended with an agreement. Rickey would sign Jackie Robinson to a contract with the Dodgers. In return, Robinson had to promise that he would not retaliate against any abuse for three years.

This was the linchpin of the Great Experiment. Rickey knew that the baseball world would look for any reason to demonize Robinson, putting an end to their plans of desegregating baseball. For the plan to work, they needed to convince the world of two things: Jackie Robinson could play baseball, and he was a gentleman worthy of praise for his talents.

Robinson sat in Rickey's office and thought about the arrangement. He understood the gravity of his decision. If the Great Experiment was a success, it would advance Robinson's entire race and the betterment of the American people. But, should the experiment fail, the baseball world may never give another Black player a chance. After some time in quiet consideration, an act that impressed Rickey greatly, Robinson agreed, and the Great Experiment began.

War on the Basepaths

Jackie Robinson began his journey towards the Brooklyn Dodgers by playing for their affiliate team in Montreal. Branch Rickey hoped that Canada was more racially enlightened than the US, giving his new player a chance to get an easy start to what would be an incredibly hard war of attrition.

That said, Robinson's time with the Montreal Royals was not without bigotry and unfair treatment. His own manager remarked that Robinson was not a human being because of his black skin. Robinson ignored the comments and compiled an impressive year with the Royals. Through his hitting, fielding, and baserunning, he drove the team to a Minor League World Series trophy. By the end of the season, Robinson's manager had changed his tune, referring to his new star as "a great ballplayer."

It became apparent to the Dodgers team that Jackie Robinson was on his way to Brooklyn. The next season, on April 15, 1947, Robinson started at first base for the Dodgers, demolishing the imaginary wall that had kept his people out of organized baseball for decades. It was a significant moment in baseball and US history and a catalyst for race reform and change in the country.

Of course, Robinson was met with resistance everywhere. Umpires would declare him out even when he clearly wasn't. Pitchers threw at his head. Baserunners slid into him on purpose. Fans wrote him death threats and hollered racist remarks during games. Teammates stayed away from in the dugout or blamed him when hotels on the road would deny the team accommodations.

In the face of the nonstop nightmare, Robinson continued to play without any altercations, proving to the world, as Branch Rickey intended, that he was a gentleman and a good ballplayer. Dodgers' fans, even those in the Whites-only section, began to fall in love with his daring baserunning and powerful swing.

His teammates, even those that had once tried to sign a petition to prevent him from joining the team, also changed sides. How could they not? Here was a man who endured more in nine innings than most had in their lifetime. Their proximity to Robinson as teammates meant that they saw and experienced everything he did. It united the Dodgers behind Robinson.

Suddenly, Jackie wasn't alone.

An American Hero

Jackie Robinson kept his word to Branch Rickey, never retaliating or striking back against those that felt so compelled to unjustly hate and threaten him because of the color of his skin. His strength and stoicism in the face of evil had a profound effect on the American psyche. It set the stage for the Civil Rights movement by maturing the nation's views on race and equality.

Dr. Martin Luther King Jr. and other Civil Rights leaders opened the door, but it was Robinson who unlocked it. Don Newcombe, Robinson's first Black teammate on the Dodgers, shared some insights on King's thoughts about the hero's influence:

> Do you know what Jackie's impact was? Well, let Martin Luther King tell you. In 1968, Martin had dinner in my house with my family. This was 28 days before he was assassinated. He said to me, "Don, I don't know what I would've done without you guys setting up the minds of people for change. You, Jackie, and Roy (Campanella) will never know how easy you made it for me to

do my job." Can you imagine that? How easy we made it for Martin Luther King!

Every year, on April 15, Major League Baseball honors Jackie Robinson's legacy. Every player wears the number 42, the only time the hallowed number is worn. Jackie Robinson Day is not a celebration of a baseball career. Sure, Robinson was a tremendous ballplayer, but so are a lot of players, past and present. These other players don't have holidays.

Major League Baseball and the US remember Jackie Robinson on this particular day because he was more than a player. Robinson was an American hero. He endured unfathomable volumes of hatred and abuse for a selfless pursuit: equality and fairness - two principles at the core of baseball and America.

Ernie Harwell once wrote, "In baseball, democracy shines its clearest. The only race that matters is the race to the bag. The creed is the rule book. And color, merely something to distinguish one team's uniform from another's." Thanks to Jack Roosevelt Robinson, these words are true.

Did You Know?

- Jackie Robinson played himself in the 1950 film *The Jackie Robinson Story*.

- Many people cite Jackie Robinson as the first Black baseball player in the major leagues. However, 60 years earlier, Moses Fleetwood Walker played for the Toledo Blue Stockings. Sadly, he didn't have the impact of Robinson on the game.

- Jackie Robinson was a four-sport athlete, with baseball low on his priority list. He only began playing for the Kansas City Monarchs in the Negro League because it offered a paying job after the war.

- There was never an official rule that kept Black players from joining an American League or National League team. Rather, it was an unspoken rule founded on a "gentleman's" agreement between owners and the baseball commissioner.

- Aside from his role in breaking baseball's color barrier, Branch Rickey also helped lay the groundwork for Major League Baseball's farm team system during his time with the St. Louis Cardinals.

- Jackie Robinson won the first-ever Rookie of the Year Award. The award is now named after him.

CHAPTER 3:

WHY WE REMEMBER ROBERTO CLEMENTE

On the 50th anniversary of Jackie Robinson breaking baseball's color barrier, Major League Baseball officially retired his uniform number across all teams. No player will wear the famous number 42 again (except on Jackie Robinson Day). If there is ever to be another uniform retired by all teams, it might be number 21 for Roberto Clemente.

Clemente's career on the diamond was outstanding. With 3,000 career hits in 18 seasons, his lifetime batting average was .317. He also helped Pittsburgh secure two World Series titles, even earning World Series MVP honors in 1971. He also had a regular season MVP award (1966), 12 Gold Gloves for outstanding fielding, four batting titles, and 15 All-Star Game invites.

Yet, Clemente's legacy is most remembered by what he did *off* the field. When he wasn't working on his baseball career, he was helping others, especially children. He set the bar, and set it high, for how athletes and celebrities should use their fame for the betterment of society. Clemente's legacy makes it difficult to say if he was a baseball player or a humanitarian first. He was equally both.

Every year, a baseball player receives the Roberto Clemente Award. It's a rare award in sports because it takes into account a player's achievements on the field *and* off. It was originally the Commissioner's Award before being renamed the Roberto Clemente Award in 1973. To understand why, you have to know the story of one of baseball's greatest humanitarians (and also a darn good ball player).

From Puerto Rico to Pittsburgh

Roberto Clemente was born in Carolina, Puerto Rico, in the Barrio San Antón. He was the youngest of his six siblings and began working from a young age to help provide for the family. His natural athleticism became apparent early, and he was a track and field star at school. Many close to the Clemente family felt he would be a future Olympian. However, he turned his focus to baseball instead.

After success in high school, he joined a local, amateur team at age 16. The Ferdinand Juncos became Clemente's team for the next two years. He excelled at multiple positions and provided good offense. He graduated into Puerto Rico's professional league just before his 18th birthday, joining the Cangrejos de Santurce.

At this time, baseball scouts were busy in Central America, tapping into these talent pools to build up Major League Baseball teams. While Clemente is known for being a Pittsburgh Pirate, it was Al Campanis, scouting for the Brooklyn Dodgers, who first spotted Clemente. He immediately recognized the raw athleticism and baseball talent, calling him "the best free-agent athlete [he'd] ever seen." At Campanis' request, the Dodgers tendered Clemente an offer. He accepted.

Even though the Dodgers gave him a contract, they ultimately lost rights to him because of the bonus rule instituted in 1947. The rule stated that a team signing a player for more than $4,000 had to keep said player on their active, 25-man roster. Clemente was not on the Dodgers roster, per the rule's stipulations. Instead, they sent him to the Montreal Royals, a Triple-A affiliate.

This was not a blunder but an intentional strategy. Brooklyn was hoping to hide Clemente's talents in Montreal, an area they knew scouts didn't frequent. They even limited his playing and practicing time to keep him out of sight of scouts.

There are many claims as to why the Dodgers didn't immediately bring Clemente to the big leagues. Buzzie Bavasi reported that it was simply to keep him out of the hands of their rivals, the New York Giants. Later in life, Bavasi said it was a race issue. The Dodgers were worried about angering fans by adding another Black player to the roster.

Despite their efforts to hide Clemente, Clyde Sukeforth from the Pittsburgh Pirates caught a glimpse of the future star and was immediately sold. Initially, Sukeforth was scouting one of Clemente's teammates, but his attention shifted to Clemente. When he left Montreal to report back to the Pirates organization, he told the Royals' manager to take care of Clemente, calling him "our boy." A year later, Clemente debuted in Pittsburgh with the Pirates.

Over the next 17 years, Pittsburgh would become Clemente's second home after Puerto Rico. Although, the transition was not as smooth as fans may think. As a half-Black and half-Latino player, he faced twice the amount of racial transgressions. Even though Jackie Robinson had broken baseball's color barrier, Black players still experienced subtle and outright racism. Clemente also caught criticism for his Puerto Rican side and heavy accent. For instance, whenever he was injured, it became the result of his "natural laziness" in the media's eyes.

Through all this criticism, Clemente rose above and became 'The Great One', as he's remembered today.

Clemente On the Field

It took a couple of years for Clemente to come into his own on the Pirates. He overcame the steady doses of racism and used the media's comments to fuel his active and aggressive styles of play on the field. By 1960, he was one of the best players in the league and a household name in Pittsburgh.

He batted above .300 for most of the season, pushing his average as high as .353. The 1960 season also saw Clemente make one of the dazzling plays he'd become known for. He caught a long Willie Mays fly ball, running into the outfield wall spectacularly in the process, but keeping hold of the ball.

Clemente's performance during the 1960 season helped the Pirates make it to the World Series. His hitting and fielding continued to shine, recording hits in every game and batting in multiple runs. These RBIs became difference-makers in the razor-close games. Ultimately, Clemente and the Pittsburgh Pirates would defeat the New York Yankees in seven games.

The 1960 season marked the first year of many that Clemente would lead the Pirates in offense and defense. He became a yearly member of the All-Star squad and consistently batted above .300 in every year except 1968. He also won 'Gold Glove' awards for his position each year.

The Pirates would reach the World Series again in 1971. This time they faced the Baltimore Orioles, a team with over 100 wins and the reigning World Series champions. Again, the Pittsburgh squad battled with the help of Clemente to reach Game 7, even after losing the first two games of the series. In the seventh and final game, Clemente hit a clutch home run to help the Pirates win the game 2-1 and claim the World Series title. He was named the World Series MVP.

The following season would be Clemente's last. He reached the milestone of 3,000 hits on September 30. It would be one of his final games.

Clemente Off the Field

Baseball history books and statisticians remember Clemente's on-field performance. While the numbers are more than enough to solidify his legacy, it was truly what Clemente did off the field that makes him a Hall of Famer. Clemente's reputation as a humanitarian spanned from Puerto Rico to Pittsburgh.

For his birth home in Puerto Rico, he used the fame and money from his baseball career to provide aid to his neighborhood and beyond. Clemente was particularly focused on opening free baseball clinics for children, believing any child with an interest in baseball should have the tools and equipment to play. He provided all of the balls, gloves, bats, and other gear with his own money.

When he worked at his clinics in the off-season, he viewed the work as both baseball and life instruction. In his own words: "I get kids together and talk about the importance of sports, the importance of being a good citizen, the importance of respecting their mother and father. Then we go to the ball field and I show them some techniques of playing baseball." Clemente's dream was to open a complex large enough that kids in Puerto Rico, especially those from low-income households, could come, stay, and learn different sports and values.

In Pittsburgh, he was a regular visitor to the children's hospital. He'd spend hours meeting with patients to boost their spirits. He also attended many local events in Pittsburgh, driving support for the city's community. Many fans fondly recall his generosity and patience when signing autographs, especially for the younger audiences.

Clemente's empathy stretched beyond Pittsburgh and Puerto Rico. He also spent time in other Latin American countries, looking for ways to improve the quality of life in the places he visited. When an earthquake devastated Nicaragua in 1972, Clemente arranged relief efforts, getting directly involved in collecting donations. In total, his community efforts raised $150,000, as well as 26 tons of supplies (food, clothes, medicine).

When reports came that these relief supplies weren't making it to the people of Nicaragua, Clemente stepped in again. He flew with the new shipment personally, hoping that his presence would deter the corrupt parties that were redirecting the supplies elsewhere.

Unfortunately, Clemente's plane crashed shortly after take-off. The plane was too overloaded with supplies and had mechanical issues that led to engine failure. Clemente and the crew perished in the crash. It marked the end of one of the greatest baseball players and humanitarians of the time.

Clemente's Spirit

Roberto Clemente's body was never recovered from the fatal plane crash, but his legacy continues to endure and inspire people today. His story offers a lasting example to current players on how to use the fame and benefits of being a Major League Baseball player to better the community and even the world.

Puerto Rico mourned their star's death for three days. The tragedy is still remembered on the island with the same clarity and sensitivity as Americans remember September 11, Pearl Harbor, or the assassination of JFK.

Shortly after Clemente's passing, the Puerto Rican government fulfilled his dream of a sports complex for children. They dedicated over 300 acres near the baseball star's home neighborhood to build The Roberto Clemente Sports City. Millions of children have participated in free clinics at this complex, including several future baseball stars, like Bernie Williams and Ivan Rodriguez.

It wouldn't be the last time a structure would bear Clemente's name. In fact, no athlete in history has more statues or monuments than the Puerto Rican star. His name has found its way on schools, streets, bridges, parks, baseball fields, and more. These dedications appear in several countries, demonstrating the expansive reach of Clemente's humanitarian efforts.

He is a national hero, a Hall of Famer, and an example of what it means to be a good person. Clemente sums himself up best. In the Puerto Rican star's own words, "I was born to play baseball," and "Any time you have an opportunity to make a difference in this world and you don't, then you are wasting your time on earth." Clemente's time on this planet may have been cut short, but he did not waste a single moment of it.

Did You Know?

- Robert Clemente's career ended with exactly 3,000 hits.

- Clemente was the first Hispanic player inducted into the Hall of Fame. He is also the first Hispanic player to win a World Series, be named MVP and World Series MVP, and many other career and seasonal records.

- Clemente is also a member of the Marine Corps Sports Hall of Fame. He was inducted posthumously in 2003.

- Clemente started his career with the Pirates wearing the number 13. Earl Smith had ownership of the soon-famous 21. When Smith retired in 1955, shortly after Clemente's career with Pittsburgh started, the Hispanic Hall of Famer took the number. He chose 21 because it was the number of letters in his full name (Roberto Clemente Walker).

- He was the first player to hit an inside-the-park grand slam in Major League Baseball. In 2022, Raimel Tapia became the second player to achieve the feat.

- No player has ever won the Roberto Clemente Award twice.

CHAPTER 4:

THE HUMBLE UPBRINGING OF BABE RUTH

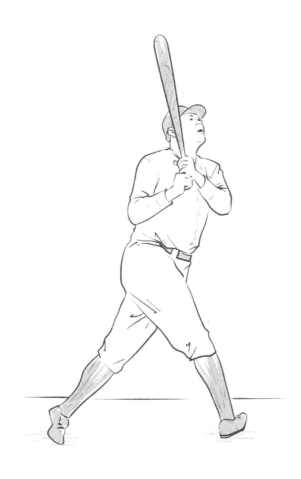

Babe Ruth is one of the most well-known figures in American sports history. He was the first true home run hitter. At the time, home runs were rare. Entire *teams* hit only a handful during a season. Suddenly, Ruth comes along and hits them at regular intervals. During the summer of 1927, Ruth hit 60 home runs, a record that stood for 34 years. (Check out chapter 6 for the story of how the record was broken.)

His home run-hitting and larger-than-life persona made Ruth a mammoth celebrity. He was beloved everywhere he went thanks to his jovial attitude and boisterous persona. Like Clemente, Ruth made a point to visit orphanages and sick children in hospitals. He rarely turned down signing autographs for young fans.

This generosity lasted until his final days. While sick in the hospital, kids would stand on the sidewalk under his window, hoping to just catch a glimpse of him. When he became too weak to stand and wave down at the children, he began signing cards and baseballs, enlisting the nursing staff to deliver them to the young fans below. When he ran out, he'd hand a nurse money and request ice cream be bought for the children.

Ruth was also charitable to teammates, often lending money and asking for no interest (or conveniently forgetting he lent the money at all). If he could help with his time or money, he would do it more times than not.

Considering this generous nature, one might assume that Ruth came from an affluent background, where money was never an issue. In reality, Ruth had incredibly humble beginnings.

St. Mary's Industrial School

There's a common myth that Babe Ruth was an orphan. While untrue, there is a tiny shred of truth to the matter. George Herman Ruth was born to a poor family. His parents worked tirelessly to provide, leaving little time for supervision for the children. Even with his parents' best efforts, only one of Babe Ruth's siblings would live past childhood.

Without the watchful eyes of his parents or the normal disciplinary action that a child might undergo when misbehaving, young Babe Ruth ran wild. Nothing his parents did to mentor him seemed to have any effect on his incorrigible nature. Ruth himself said later in life he rarely attended school in his early years. Instead, he spent most days running amok in the streets of Baltimore with other delinquent and unsupervised youths.

With his father operating a saloon, Ruth would steal beers at the age of five or six. He'd also chew tobacco, fight with other children, throw things at people walking by (usually policemen looking for truant youths), and much more. It was abhorrent behavior for a boy of only six.

At age seven, his parents decided they didn't have the time, fortitude, or ability to properly raise their ruffian son. With the hopes of providing the best chance for the wayward boy, they decided to send him to nearby St. Mary's Industrial School. It was a last-ditch effort to establish stability for their son.

St. Mary's was part orphanage (hence the misconception that Ruth was an orphan), part trade school, and part reform school. It was run by the Xaverian Brothers, who were strict in their discipline and molding of the boys in their care. The boys performed every task conceivable at the school, from cooking and cleaning to making clothes or repairing the school.

It was at St. Mary's that Ruth first started learning baseball. His mentor, Brother Matthias, introduced him to the sport that would lead him to eternal greatness. Brother Matthias also became the father figure Ruth needed. It was an odd pairing considering Brother Matthias was the chief disciplinarian and Ruth was the chief of misbehavior.

When it came to baseball, Ruth attributed much of his skill to Brother Matthias. He even mirrored his mentor's hitting and playing styles. In one account, Ruth stated, "I think I was born as a hitter the first day I ever saw [Brother Matthias] hit a baseball." It was also Brother Matthias who first turned Ruth to pitching.

The story goes that Ruth was antagonizing his team's pitcher because he had given up several runs. In response, Brother Matthias put young Babe on the mound in relief. It was an attempt to show him what it's like to be in a pitcher's shoes. He may have even intended to embarrass Ruth. Instead, the growing baseball player flourished on the mound and swiftly became the team's pitcher.

It was an early step in his journey to becoming a baseball legend. Ruth never underestimated the impact St. Mary's and Brother Matthias had on his life. When the school caught fire in 1919, Ruth (now a seasoned baseball player with the New York Yankees) stepped in to raise money for repairs and rebuilding.

The Beginning of The Babe

Word of Babe Ruth's baseball talent reached the professional ears of Jack Dunn, owner and manager of the Baltimore Orioles (a minor league team at the time). The exact circumstances around Ruth signing with the Orioles aren't entirely clear. There are various accounts of the story. At best guess, Dunn saw Ruth pitching during an all-star game between St. Mary's and another Xaverian institute and approached him with a contract.

Dunn is why George Herman Ruth became "Babe." Teammates would refer to him as "Dunn's Babe" because he was the manager's project player. Dunn also became his legal guardian. This "project" wasn't strictly the sculpting of a baseball prodigy. Ruth's life at St. Mary's kept him incredibly sheltered. His trip to spring training in North Carolina was the first time he left his small bubble of Baltimore.

Ruth had no concept of how to act in public. Despite the disciplinary efforts of St. Mary's and years of growing up (now around 19 years of age), he was still a child at heart. This was a demeanor he'd never really shake, even as an adult, and added to his lovable nature in the eyes of fans. Dunn had to teach Ruth how to act when riding a train, dining in a restaurant, visiting other cities, checking into hotels, and more.

When Dunn's Baltimore Orioles ran into financial hardships, the owner sold the contracts of his best players, including Ruth's. Babe Ruth was sent to the Boston Red Sox. In Boston, Ruth didn't have Dunn or Brother Matthias for guidance. He frequently had altercations with teammates who didn't like the oversized personality of the rookie. He also expanded his tastes to include fine food, liquor, cigars, and women.

Nonetheless, Boston was a transformative place for Ruth. He was playing on the biggest stage and pitching well enough to be in the Red Sox starting rotation. As a pitcher, he was kept out of the lineup often, which Ruth detested.

He wanted more opportunities to play, especially to bat. Ed Barrow was hesitant at first. Ruth was a dominant pitcher, possibly the best left-hander in the game. Allowing him to play another position on days he wasn't on the mound heightened the risk of injury.

Ultimately, Barrow gave in. His change of heart was primarily financial. Crowds were bigger on days that Ruth pitched and part of that draw was his hitting. Barrow also felt Ruth would fall out of love with hitting once he fell into a slump and would want to return to pitching exclusively. That never happened. Ruth was now one of baseball's best pitchers and greatest hitters.

The following year, Ruth played a central role in securing a World Series win for the Red Sox. Not only did he pitch one out shy of 30 scoreless innings (a record that stood for over 40 years), but he remained in the lineup as a hitter, playing defensive positions as well. It was one of Ruth's crowning career achievements.

The year after the 1918 Red Sox World Series win, Ruth's contract was sold to the New York Yankees. Ruth's contract went for $100,000 (around $2M today); it was the most anyone had ever paid for a baseball player. Even with the king's ransom paid, many sportswriters at the time suggested New York pulled off the heist of the century by acquiring Ruth. History proved these individuals correct.

The Red Sox had won five World Series titles between 1903 and 1919, the year Ruth's contract went to the Yankees. After this transaction, they wouldn't win it all again until 2004. Meanwhile, the Yankees, a non-competitor for those first 16 years, won the American League Pennant seven times with Ruth and claimed the first four of their now-27 World Series titles.

Home Runs and Hot Dogs

Once with the Yankees, Ruth became a full-time offensive player. He rarely pitched again. Although, he did get the win every time he took the mound for the Yankees, no matter how long it had been since he pitched. This shift gave Babe Ruth, the opportunity to become the slugger everyone knows today.

Ruth's proficiency at hitting home runs was unprecedented. In his first appearance in May with the Yankees, he set a major league record for home runs in a single month. He then broke his own record the following month. It wasn't just volume but distance. He hit tape-measure home runs at every ballpark the Yankees visited. It became such a spectacle that he also became responsible for attendance records at most major ballparks.

By the end of the 1920 season, he had hit 54 home runs, a new record. His high mark didn't just break the old record.

It demolished it! Better yet, Ruth hit even *more* home runs the following year, setting the bar to 59. He quickly smashed Roger Connor's career home run mark. The Babe was just getting started.

His proclivity for huge home runs matched his massive aura. He took to New York City (and NYC to him) like mustard to a hot dog. He wasn't just another celebrity; he was *the* superstar of the biggest city in America. This status expanded far beyond the geographical limitations of the city. He was known everywhere and anywhere he went.

His rise to superstardom couldn't have come at a better time. America was in the Roaring Twenties, a time of jazz music, dancing, promiscuity, city-living, and lavishness - all things that appealed greatly to Ruth. The Roaring Twenties also saw the rise of automobiles, films with sound, telephones, and many other electrical appliances - more stuff that Ruth would fall in love with, especially films.

As the years fell off the calendar, Ruth's celebrity status only grew exponentially. He was treated like royalty with free meals and drinks. Teammates would recall following him back to his hotel suite to find tubs of cold beer, boxes of cigars, and more - all given gratis. It seemed excessive, but Ruth was also excessive. The same teammate memories would also recall him consuming most of the gifts in a single night.

Ruth's gluttonous nature eventually caught up to him in the infamous "bellyache heard 'round the world" event. It was the spring of 1925. By this time, Ruth and the Yankees had won a World Series title and several AL Pennants. Ruth was coming off another unbelievable year, hitting 46 home runs and winning the AL batting title with a .378 average.

However, Ruth's weight was nearly as high as his career home run total at the time (284 home runs). He collapsed in his NY hotel room one afternoon and was rushed to the hospital. The cause of his condition has never clearly been identified. One sportswriter reported it was the result of scarfing down too many hot dogs and sodas before that day's game. Thus, the legend of the "bellyache heard 'round the world" started.

Thanks to bellyaches, or whatever it may have been, 1925 was one of Ruth's worse years. He quickly rebounded the next year, getting back into shape and entering the season surrounded by newly acquired talent.

This was the start of the Yankees' Murderers' Row lineup, largely considered to be one of the best teams ever assembled (Babe Ruth, Lou Gehrig, Earle Combs, Tony Lazzeri, Bob Meusel, just to name a few players). With this high-performance team, the Yankees took back-to-back World Series titles in 1927 and 1928.

The 1927 campaign was the year that Ruth hit 60 home runs - his greatest total yet. It was also one of the best seasons for the New York Yankees ever. Ruth wasn't the only player swatting home runs at a frequent clip. Teammate Lou Gehrig kept pace with him for most of the season, ending with 47. Overall, the team won 110 games, a league record. They clinched the pennant with ease. The World Series wasn't much harder, as they swept over the Pirates in four games.

Ascension

The 1927 season solidified Babe Ruth's seat atop the Mount Olympus of baseball. He had arguably the greatest baseball season for a player and his team. Sure, Roger Maris hit one more home run and also went on to win the series, but he wasn't beloved like Ruth. Mark McGwire, Sammy Sosa, Barry Bonds, Aaron Judge - none of them had the team success.

You could take the 1927 campaign on its own and Ruth would still be one of the greats. It didn't matter what he did before or after. Factoring in the before and after only furthers the gap between Ruth and other baseball legends. It's the reason that his legacy, even almost a century later, transcends baseball. He's the baseball name most deserving to be associated with titles like legend and icon.

The longevity of The Babe has a lot to do with when he played. He hit 60 home runs when most teams only hit half that, or less. Home run hitters just didn't exist. Seeing a home run at the ballpark was a bonus, not the main attraction. There was no record before Ruth. Thus, he is eternally tied to one of baseball's most coveted and exciting single-season records.

Babe Ruth is different from every player, before and after. He may not be the greatest player ever, but he's the greatest *something*. His life and baseball career are unique and incomparable; it's impossible to put him in a single box. He is a colossus, a behemoth, a titan, a king, a prince, a wizard, a sultan, and the Bambino.

Did You Know?

- There is no other player with more nicknames than Ruth. His list of monikers includes "Babe," "Bam," "the Big Bam," "the Big Fellow," "the Sultan of Swat," "the Great Bambino," "the Sanchem of Slug," "the Prince of Pounders," "the Wizard of Whack," "Wali of Wallop," "the Behemoth of Bust," "Jidge," "the King of Swing," "the Titan of Terror," "the Colossus of Clout," "the King of Crash," and others.

- Ruth holds the record for most innings pitched in a World Series game. During Game 2 of the 1916 World Series, he pitched a 14-inning complete game. Considering how closely today's teams monitor pitch counts and times through the lineup, it is a record that will never be broken.

- Babe Ruth appeared in 10 films during his life. In the 1920s, he appeared in *Headin' Home* (1920), *Babe Comes Home* (1927), and *Speedy*. In 1932 alone, five short films featured the famous slugger, including *Slide, Babe, Slide, Fancy Curves, Over the Fence, Perfect Control,* and *Just Pals*. He was also in the short film *Home Run on the Keys* in 1937. His final and most famous film, *The Pride of the Yankees*, detailed the life of his late teammate Lou Gehrig.

- Ruth long believed his birthday was February 7, 1894. He had both the day and year wrong, a truth he discovered when applying for a passport to visit Japan in 1934. His actual birth date was February 6, 1895.

- Babe Ruth is part of one of the weirdest combined no-hitters in history. After walking the leadoff batter, Ruth became enraged by umpire Ray Morgan's strike zone. He was removed from the game after arguing and starting a physical altercation with the umpire. Ernie Shore had to come into the game to replace the rejected Ruth. Shore threw nine hitless innings.

- Babe Ruth hit three home runs in two separate postseason games. The first happened in Game 4 of the 1926 World Series. He did it again in Game 4 of the 1928 World Series. Reggie Jackson, Albert Pujols, and Pablo Sandoval have each hit three dingers in a World Series game, but none have done it twice like Ruth.

CHAPTER 5:

MARIANO RIVERA'S RAGS TO RICHES STORY

For many years in the 90s and early 2000s, playing the New York Yankees felt like an eight-inning affair, rather than a nine-inning one. This was all thanks to one player: Mariano Rivera. Rivera is the greatest closer in the game. He was so dominant that when opposing teams heard his choice song, *Enter Sandman*, playing, it sent a message: the game is about to be put to rest.

His Metallica entrance music suggests a player with equal parts of rock and roll. This was not Mariano Rivera. On the mound, he was focused, cold, and the embodiment of grace under pressure. He went after batters with an emotionless precision of a hitman with a target in the scope.

Adding to his assassin-like allure was his singular choice in weaponry. Most pitchers have an arsenal of pitches at their disposal. They change their pitch types to leave the hitter guessing. Will the next pitch be another fastball? Maybe a changeup? Slider? Splitter? With Rivera, there was no guessing. Like James Bonds' trusty Walter PPK, Rivera only needed his fastball.

Standard logic would suggest that this put Rivera at a disadvantage on the mound. With only one pitch to throw, everyone knows what's about to happen. Plus, the batter has to see the pitch at least three times in an at-bat. This gives them multiple opportunities to see it and make adjustments. So, why was Rivera still so successful, despite the odds seemingly in the hitter's favor?

Hitter Mike Sweeney best puts Rivera's magic into perspective. "Sure, you know what's coming," he said. "But you know what's coming in horror movies, too." You still get scared and jump. That's what Rivera's fastball was like - an incoming horror movie propelled at 96 MPH.

Calling it a fastball doesn't quite do the pitch justice. After all, Excalibur isn't just another sword. Rivera's fastball dove to the left at the very last minute, closely resembling a cutter. But even that title doesn't fit. Other pitchers throw cutters. Rivera's was something different, perhaps otherworldly. The man himself stated he "learned the pitch from God."

In his memoir, Rivera explains that he didn't work on his pitch. It just sort of happened. One day, his fastball spiked impossibly in velocity. It later adopted its signature cut, which worried the pitcher at first. He couldn't seem to throw straight anymore. He had yet to realize that he had just acquired one of the deadliest pitches in history.

The First Divine Intervention

Mariano Rivera was born in Panama and lived in Puerto Caimito. It was a fishing village with little to offer its residents. When Rivera and his boyhood friends would play baseball, they relied on cardboard for gloves, rocks wrapped in fishing line for balls, and branches as bats. He wouldn't receive a proper glove until he was 12 years old.

It's hard to picture humbler beginnings for someone destined to become one of the greatest to ever play baseball.

While Rivera enjoyed baseball, he treated it as a hobby, even as he got older. Most of his time was spent working on a commercial fishing boat captained by his father. The work was hard and dangerous. The future pitcher had dreams of being a mechanic and saved his money to open his own auto body shop. It seemed impossible to imagine that his baseball hobby would lead him anywhere.

He was good enough at his baseball "hobby" to secure a spot on the Vaqueros amateur team in nearby Panamá Oeste. He started playing shortstop and was even scouted once but didn't stand out as an MLB-caliber player. The next season, Rivera took the mound for the first time. He was called in to relieve a teammate. It was the first time he'd pitched, but he naturally excelled.

A few weeks later, he was invited to a tryout camp held by the Yankees in Panama City. His teammates had reached out to a Yankees scout to rave about Rivera's newfound role as a pitcher. Despite his low velocity and lack of experience or formal training, the scouting staff viewed him as naturally gifted with a smooth pitching motion. He was a raw talent that could, maybe, be molded into a professional big leaguer.

On February 17, 1990, the New York Yankees signed Rivera. His signing bonus - reported as $2,500 - was roughly what the young Panamanian made in an entire year of fishing. It was a life-changing event that, like developing his cutter, felt divine to Rivera.

Not only did his teammate, a typically sturdy pitcher, crumble on the **mound** and allow Rivera to assume a new role, but his performance that day felt almost out of body. "I got results that were way beyond my physical abilities," he states in his autobiography.

That same year, Rivera had taken to studying the Bible again, at the urging of a family member.

The Second Divine Intervention

Mariano Rivera's minor league career started well, despite the pitcher suffering from severe homesickness. Rivera didn't speak English and could only communicate with family through letters (Puerto Caimito had no phone lines).

In his first season in the Gulf Coast League, he allowed only one earned run in 52 innings. He also had a seven-inning no-hitter in the final game of the season. His impressive record that season elevated his status from a fringe prospect to someone of note.

The next season, pitching in Class A ball, Rivera had a 4-9 record. While this doesn't sound great on paper, his ERA stayed solid at 2.75, and he had a high ratio of strikeouts to walks, drawing attention from New York Yankees manager Buck Showalter. He continued this performance the following year in Advanced-A, where he would have a 5-3 record with a 2.28 ERA. He walked only five batters in almost 60 innings pitched, showcasing great control and the ability to manage pressure.

Rivera's season in the Advanced-A league was marred slightly by injury. Not only did he start the season with elbow stiffness, missing several games, but he eventually underwent surgery in late August. Luckily, it wasn't a ligament tear and only needed repairing, which saved the young pitcher from requiring a more serious procedure.

Rivera's future as a New York Yankee caught another lucky break when he went untouched in the 1992 expansion draft. This was a special draft intended to help two new teams, the Florida Marlins and Colorado Rockies, build their teams. Essentially, these new clubs were allowed to draft players from existing teams. However, those teams could protect individuals on their 40-man roster, preventing them from the selection process.

The Yankees did not protect Mariano Rivera. He was eligible to be drafted by the Rockies or Marlins. Luckily, he wasn't, but it was close. A stipulation of the expansion draft was a team couldn't lose more than one player per round. Florida planned to take Rivera in the third and final round, but the Rockies selected Brad Ausmus from the Yankees. This meant no more Yankees could be taken. Rivera was safe.

It may not have been as life-changing of an event as his initial signing with the Yankees. Yet, when you consider Mariano Rivera's legacy in pinstripes, avoiding being signed by the Florida Marlins is an incredibly significant event. It would have changed his trajectory dramatically.

The Third Divine Intervention

Mariano Rivera's path to the Bronx continued with rehabilitation from his elbow surgery. His 1993 season was limited, getting short pitching performances when possible. Despite the restricted workload, Rivera maintained his typical numbers. He ended the season with around 43 innings pitched and a 2.08 ERA. He walked only 16 batters, showcasing his typical control. He'd be fully recovered by the 1994 season and ready for a normal workload.

Early into the '94 season, Rivera moved up to Double-A. He quickly became the best starter on the team, graduating to Triple-A in the same season. The Panamanian ended the year with a 10-2 record and a 3.09 ERA between Double and Triple-A. The stiffer competition in Triple-A certainly caught up to Rivera. His ERA in this league jumped to 5.81

in six starts. It was a small sample size, but it was a sign of coming struggles against more experienced players.

Even with the jump in ERA, Rivera was considered a top prospect in the Yankees organization. The 1995 season was the first time New York Yankees fans would see Rivera on the big stage. It was not a great showing. In his first outing, Rivera survived just 3 and 1/3 innings, allowing five earned runs. His ERA was an abysmal 10.20 after five starts. He was sent back to Triple-A less than a month after coming up.

There were talks of trading Rivera in a package of players to acquire David Wells from the Detroit Tigers. He wasn't seen as much of an asset - 25 years of age, elbow surgery, a high ERA at the MLB level, etc. The assessment changed on June 26. Not only did Rivera pitch a five-inning, no-hit shutout (the game was called due to rain), but his pitch velocity miraculously jumped. He was pitching 6 MPH faster than his typical average, seemingly out of nowhere.

The spike in velocity was so dramatic that Gene Michael, the Yankees general manager, didn't believe initial reports and requested the radar gun be checked. When Rivera's pitching speed was confirmed, he no longer became a trade piece. Rivera was reinserted back into the New York Yankees rotation. His first returning start was dominant. He struck out 11 batters in eight scoreless innings, further solidifying himself as a valuable asset to the future of the Yankees.

By the end of the 1995 regular season, Rivera had ups and downs. He finished with more wins than losses, but his 5.51 ERA was still troubling. The New York Yankees had made it to the playoffs that year. They turned to Rivera for relief pitching in the ALDS against the Seattle Mariners. He pitched over five innings of scoreless baseball and looked untouchable. It changed his role in the Yankees for good, shifting from a starter to a relief pitcher.

Enter Sandman

Mariano Rivera's role in the 1996 season was as a setup pitcher for John Wetteland, the current closer. Rivera would come in to close games around the seventh or eighth inning. If necessary, Wetteland would secure the save in the ninth. The duo worked so well that when the Yankees were leading games after the sixth inning, they had a near-unbeatable record of 70 wins and just three losses.

Wetteland was elite but Rivera was untouchable. He had a stretch of 26 scoreless innings in a row, including 15 consecutive hitless innings. He ended the regular season with an ERA of 2.09. He also set a Yankees record for strikeouts by a relief pitcher. It was one of the best seasons by a reliever ever.

Rivera's dominance continued in the postseason. He let up just one run in just over 14 innings of pitching. His effort helped the Yankees win their first World Series title since 1978. It also solidified his permanent position on the team. The Yankees chose not to re-sign Wetteland after the season. They had found their new closer.

The 1997 season opened up a little rocky for Rivera; in his first six opportunities, he failed to get the save three times. Yet, once the season started rolling, he found his comfort in the new role and his excellence continued. After blowing those three saves early in the season, he'd only miss the mark seven times the rest of the year. The Yankees would make it to the postseason, but lose to Cleveland in the ALDS.

The New York Yankees won the World Series each year from 1998 to 2000, solidifying the team as one of the great dynasties in sports. The stretch also distinguished Rivera as one of the great closers of the game and an integral part of the Yankees. During this stretch is also when the closer started to build his identity. It was the time he discovered the signature cutter and started walking out to Metallica's *Enter Sandman*.

Rivera's prowess on the mound also meant another thing: more money. During salary arbitration after the 1998 season, he received a $4.25M salary. A year later, it jumped again to $7.25M per year. It's a large salary for anyone; it was also one of the highest arbitration amounts awarded in baseball. For Rivera, who'd made $50 a week in Panama, it was astronomical.

Longevity

There is a mountain of accolades, records, blow-your-mind stats, and clutch moments that help define Mariano Rivera's legacy. He is the all-time save leader (652 career saves) and finished more games (952) than any other player in history. He also had more saves over consecutive seasons than other relievers, speaking to his consistency on the mound. This earned Rivera invites to 13 All-Star games, earning the All-Star MVP in one.

Rivera's continuous dominance helped propel the Yankees to many postseasons and World Series appearances (including five titles). He had an 8-1 record in the playoffs, including 42 saves - a postseason record and more than twice the next closest player. He left the game with other postseason records for consecutive scoreless innings (33 and 1/3), consecutive save conversions (23), and games pitched (96).

His most impressive postseason track record is how difficult he was to score against. He had a 0.70 ERA in postseason games. In the 96 games he pitched against playoff teams, only 11 batters managed to score. 'If you score on Rivera in the playoffs...keep the ball,' many players would joke. More people have walked on the moon than have scored on Rivera in the postseason.

Joe Torre, the Yankees manager, said it best about Rivera's postseason performance. "Let's face it; the regular season for Mo is great, but that's the cupcakes and the ice cream. What separates him from everybody else is what he's done in the postseason."

Torre's sentiments are shared by many players who played alongside or against Rivera. Trevor Hoffman, number two on the all-time save list, said, "[Rivera] will go down as the best reliever in the game." Writer, Tom Verducci, took this a step further, "Rivera is definitively the best at his position by a wider margin than any player, at any position, in the history of baseball. There is Rivera, a gulf, and then every other closer."

Did You Know?

- During his retirement year, the Minnesota Twins gifted Mariano Rivera a rocking chair made out of bats broken by his infamous cutter.

- In 1993 when Rivera was recovering from UCL surgery, he had a limited pitch count throwing for the Greensboro Hornets. Derek Jeter, future Yankees captain and long-time teammate of Rivera, had the job of counting his pitches to ensure he didn't exceed his limit.

- Mariano Rivera pitched a "hidden" no-hitter by throwing nine hitless innings over three consecutive appearances. He went on to pitch 14 hitless innings before Tony Phillips of the White Sox notched a single.

- Rivera pitched the final out in four World Series wins (1998, 1999, 2000, and 2009), double the next closest pitchers. He has also closed out 16 total postseason series.

- Mariano Rivera was the last player to wear the number 42. Major League Baseball officially retired the number in 1997 to honor Jackie Robinson's legacy. Rivera was allowed to continue wearing the number for the remainder of his career.

- The famous closer had plans to retire from baseball early and pursue a higher calling to become a minister. He opted to stay in baseball.

CHAPTER 6:

MICKEY MANTLE AND ROGER MARIS HUNT FOR 61 HOME RUNS

Author Bill Bryson's book *One Summer* chronicles several major events that took place in the summer of 1927. The book was the result of a lifetime of research. Bryson realized that a lot of interesting *stuff* happened in just one summer: Charles Lindbergh flew across the Atlantic; The Great Mississippi Flood happened; and Babe Ruth hit 60 home runs.

The summer of 1961 had a lot of similarities. Instead of Lindbergh braving the cross-Atlantic flight, Yuri Gagarin becomes the first human to enter outer space. While not as devastating as the Mississippi flood, Hurricane Carla wreaked havoc in Texas and claimed 43 lives. And, teammates Roger Maris and Mickey Mantle pursued Babe Ruth's season home run record.

The Maris-Mantle home run race captivated the country that summer. It would have been enough for one player to approach Ruth's record. In 1961, there were two, both teammates on the Yankees. Enter almost any diner or general store in 1961 and you'd witness someone coming in and hollering, "Did Mantle hit one? What about Maris?" It didn't matter if you liked baseball or not. It became a matter of pop culture at the time.

Its hold on America's attention had less to do about baseball, Ruth, or record-breaking efforts. It became the talk of the country because of how the drama unfolded. It was an epic tale with suspense, tragedy, glory, unexpected twists, and more storytelling elements. The result was a captivating saga told throughout the summer of 1961.

The M&M Boys

Mickey Mantle had been the star of the New York Yankees for several years before the start of the 1961 season. The Oklahoma-born player was beloved for his larger-than-life persona and gritty style of play. Mantle could do it all, from base running and fielding to hitting balls with blazing velocity. He was equal parts a baseball player and an American icon.

Roger Maris was a newcomer to the New York Yankees, previously playing for Kansas City and Cleveland. Yankees fans were excited to have another excellent player on the team, but these positive sentiments didn't last long. Maris quickly became seen as an interloper when the home run race began to pick up steam. He was encroaching on Mantle's chance for immortality in baseball's history.

Babe Ruth was a Yankee himself. If anyone was going to break his single-season home run mark, it should be another Yankee as cherished as The Babe. Despite the pinstripes on his uniform, Maris wasn't a "true Yankee" yet. He was a newcomer and still an outsider.

The media leaned into this conflict, championing Mantle and denouncing Maris. There were even stories circulating that the two players didn't get along, giving fans even more fodder to dislike Maris. There was never any such conflict. In fact, the M&M boys, as they became known, even shared an apartment, together with another Yankee teammate.

No matter how much emphasis the media and fans put on the supposed rivalry, Mantle and Maris resisted. As the season chugged on, Maris faced increasingly negative responses from fans and media. At its most extreme, fans booed and threw debris onto the field (sometimes at Maris).

At his lowest points, Maris relied on two people to help him keep his sanity: his wife and Mickey Mantle. "I'm going nuts, Mick," he said to his teammate and home run competitor. "I can't stand much more of this."

The Race Is On

No one anticipates a record-breaking season. The thought of two teammates racing to topple the same record in a season? Only a fiction writer could have concocted that storyline! That said, there was plenty of buzz prior to the 1961 season about the home run prowess of the M&M boys.

In 1960, Maris had his first year with the Yankees and hit 39 home runs. Mantle hit 40. So, there was some speculation about who would hit more in 1961, but it wasn't until around June that talks of usurping Ruth began.

Maris didn't find his form until late May. He was struggling at the plate with only three home runs and a .218 average, drawing boos from fans that expected more from the player. Most sources claim it was Yankees president Dan Topping that got Maris on track, telling him to ignore the fans and the slump and focus on hitting home runs. Maris obliged and quickly added nine dingers to his total by the close of the month. By the end of June, he had hit 27.

Mantle may have gotten off to a hotter start, but his end-of-June total was two behind Maris. His performance spiked in July, hitting seven home runs in eight games. Then, a slumping Maris responded by finding his stride yet again. He'd swat four home runs in a single day against the Boston Red Sox, putting his total at 40. The same day, Mantle hit his 37th-long ball.

The race continued, neck-and-neck, back and forth. Maris hit 41, but two days later Mantle reached 43. By the middle of August, the pair were tied at 45 home runs each. They were ahead of Ruth's pace, and it became increasingly apparent that *someone* was going to be the new single-season home run king.

In an article appearing in *Life* magazine, probability experts reported that the likelihood of one of the two players (or both) breaking the record was 60%. Of course, probability projections can't predict certain factors, like illness and injury. By the end of the home run race, Mickey Mantle would experience both.

The Un-Jolly Roger Is Alone

It's unclear exactly when Mickey Mantle became sick or what the affliction was. The story seemed to change depending on who reported it. The reality was that his performance started to skid by mid-September. He was slumping more than he wasn't. The virus, or cold, or respiratory infection was taking its toll on the Oklahoma-born player.

On September 14, he declared, "I can't make it - not even in 162 games." At this time, Mantle had only made his ongoing illness known to a handful of people. He tried an injection to help combat the suspected virus. Unfortunately, the needle hit his hip bone and exacerbated the situation. Mantle had to be hospitalized in the final days of the season. His home run total sat at 54.

Roger Maris was suddenly alone in the home run race.

It was perhaps the worst-case scenario for the press. Mantle was naturally likable and easy-going in the face of cameras and questions. Maris, on the other hand, was reserved, shy, and didn't like the spotlight. The media spun his disinterest to make him unlikeable. They had taken to calling him the "Not-so-jolly Roger."

Now the same sources that had vilified Maris had no other character left for the home run race story that had been captivating audiences all summer. Maris himself was not handling his main character role well. No matter what the outcome, breaking the record or not, Maris felt the press would sabotage him in some manner. The immense pressure was causing him to lose sleep and his hair. It was an impossible situation.

His one solace from all the hoopla was playing baseball. The pressure of the record never seemed to impact Maris' ability to pursue it. "The only time Roger can relax is during a ballgame," said teammate Bob Cerv.

There were five games left in the season, all home games. Maris' home run total was at 59, meaning he'd need just two more to tie and then break Ruth's record. The record-tying home run came against Baltimore on September 26. Then, in the last game of the season, Maris hit number 61, surpassing Ruth and putting the whole ordeal to rest.

Asterisks

Roger Maris was not universally accepted as the new home run single-season king. There was one caveat that many individuals would continue to cite, attempting to preserve Ruth's status as the home run season leader. Because the American League had added two new teams, the Ruth-era schedule of 154 games increased to 162.

In July, just as talks of a record-breaking home run race began, MLB Commissioner (and close friend of the late Babe Ruth) Ford Frick issued a statement that players would have to set any record in the first 154 games. Records set in the 162-game span would be in their own category.

Frick later remarked that he never ordered any asterisk on the Maris record, but that's essentially what happened. It wasn't until 1991 that the 154-game and 162-game record books merged into one, giving Maris the record for the foreseeable future.

That future, as it turned out, wasn't very long. In 1998, there was another home run race. Mark McGwire of the St. Louis Cardinals and Sammy Sosa of the Chicago Cubs hit mammoth home runs throughout the spring and summer. It brought attention back to baseball after a 1994 strike ended the season prematurely.

On September 8, McGwire hit his 62nd home run of the season, establishing himself as the new leader. Sosa had 58 round-trippers by this date. He too would pass Maris, but a week later. McGwire held his lead over Sosa for most of the remaining season. Sosa edged up by one home run with only days left in the season. McGwire then entered the home run hitting the equivalent of a mad dash for the finish line, clubbing five in three of the final games. The race ended with two names at the top of the single-season home run list: McGwire at 70 and Sosa, 66.

Three years later, Barry Bonds would surpass both players, hitting 73 home runs in the 2001 campaign. Many fans place a similar black mark on all three players' records because of the rampant steroid use at the time. Sosa and Bonds were both named in the Mitchell Report, baseball's official investigation into the issue. McGwire, who was not named in any investigations, admitted his steroid use in 2010.

In a game defined by numbers and statistics, the single-season home run record is debated with everything but.

Did You Know?

- Mickey Mantle and Roger Maris hold the record for combined home runs by a pair of teammates in a season. The record was previously set by Lou Gehrig and Babe Ruth.

- In 2022, Aaron Judge hit 62 home runs as a member of the New York Yankees, passing Maris as the new franchise leader.

- Maris remained bitter towards Yankees fans and New York media because of how he was treated during the home run race. He refused to attend events at Yankee Stadium for many years, even vowing he wouldn't return. When he did, he was moved by the overwhelming support of fans in attendance.

- There are four Yankees players on the list for most home runs in a season - Giancarlo Stanton, Aaron Judge, Roger Maris, and Babe Ruth.

- Neither Mantle nor Maris was alive to see the 61-home run mark bested.

- Roger Maris was ready to retire from baseball by 1967. He was playing for the St. Louis Cardinals at the time when the team owner offered an Anheuser-Busch beer distributorship if Maris stayed one more year. He stayed and the distributorship became Maris' lucrative post-baseball career.

CHAPTER 7:

HENRY "HAMMERIN' HANK" AARON BREAKS A HOME RUN RECORD

Today, Henry Aaron, or Hank Aaron as he's commonly known, is revered as one of the greatest players ever. He holds all-time career records for RBIs and total bases. He was an All-Star in every season but his first and last (25 in total). He is also number two for career home runs. That home run record is the crux of this story.

Hank Aaron's career spanned from 1954 to 1976, meaning his career started seven years after Jackie Robinson broke baseball's color barrier. By Aaron's rookie year, the major leagues had seen several stars make the jump from the Negro Leagues. The list includes several players from the Hall of Fame, including Monte Irvin, Satchel Paige, Larry Doby, Roy Campanella, Willie Mays, and others.

With such great talent appearing on major league teams, many fans had gotten over the unspoken Jim Crow-ism that kept Blacks out of organized baseball. It's hard to hate a player that helps your team win and succeed. As Jackie Robinson taught the world, baseball was the perfect agency to help end segregation.

Yet, Hank Aaron faced a heightened level of racism reminiscent of the struggles Robinson had to overcome to change the game forever. The reason Aaron experienced so much hatred? He threatened to break the career home run record - Babe Ruth's career home run record.

Fifty Dollars

Hank Aaron's early childhood is a story reminiscent of Mariano Rivera or Satchel Paige. He was even born in Mobile, Alabama, the same as Paige. Aaron grew up poor, without money for baseball equipment. His mother tried to dissuade him from playing baseball. She encouraged him to go to college and pursue a professional career.

Aaron only had the heart and mind to be a baseball player. He opted to ignore studying and instead practiced batting by hitting bottle caps with sticks. His high school didn't even have a baseball team, leaving Aaron to join a semi-pro team, the Mobile Black Bears. He would play alongside grown men rather than kids of his own age. Ed Scott, the man responsible for signing him to the Black Bears, remembers his early days on the team:

> He was as green as he could be. He stood up there at the plate upright, no crouch at all, and the other team figured he wasn't ready. The pitcher tried to get a fastball by him, and he hit a line drive that banged against the old tin fence they had around the outfield other there - nearly put the ball through the fence. They walked him the rest of the time.

At age 17, Aaron received an offer from the Indianapolis Clowns of the Negro American League. It was with the

Clowns that he met Dewey Griggs, a scout for the Boston Braves. Griggs was the one who encouraged Aaron to change his batting grip. Up until this time, the young player was batting cross-handed as a righty, meaning his left hand was on top, instead of the right, as is traditional. Aaron hit a home run that day.

He spent only a few months in a Clowns uniform before receiving an offer from the Boston Braves, at the urging of Griggs. In 26 games in the Negro League, he hit five home runs, 33 RBIs, 41 hits, and swiped nine bags. His batting average was .366.

Interestingly, Aaron also received an offer from the New York Giants. His reason for choosing the Braves as purely monetary. "I had the Giants' contract in my hand," Aaron remembered later, "But the Braves offered fifty dollars a month more. That's the only thing that kept Willie Mays and me from being teammates - fifty dollars."

Before Giants fans lose their lunch over what could have been, it's worth noting the Braves would have happily spent more. The Braves' GM at the time, John Quinn, said they felt Aaron was a $100,000 player.

Rise to Stardom

Henry Aaron started his professional baseball career with the Eau Clair Bears, a Class-C farm team for the

Braves. He exceeded expectations in his first year and was the unanimous pick for Rookie of the Year in the league. The next season, he graduated to the team's Class-A affiliate, the Jacksonville Braves.

In Class-A, Aaron led the league in several batting categories, including runs, hits, doubles, RBIs, and total bases. "Henry Aaron led the league in everything except hotel accommodations," remarked one writer, hinting at the constant racism the young player faced as one of the few Black players in the league.

Aaron had a busy off-season. Not only did he meet and marry his first wife, but he also traveled to Puerto Rico to further hone his baseball skills. Until now, Aaron had played second base. In Puerto Rico, he made the shift to the outfield after his manager there noted he could catch fly balls with ease and had the arm to rifle the ball back to the infield.

His stellar performance across each league prompted the now-Milwaukee Braves to invite the young player to the team's spring training. When Bobby Thomson injured his ankle in a slide, the spot became Aaron's. At the end of spring, the Braves offered Aaron a contract to play in the majors. He quickly collected his first hit (and his first home run) by mid-April. His rookie season with the Braves saw him bat .280 with 13 home runs before hurting his ankle in early September.

With his rocky rookie year behind him, Aaron swiftly fell into the groove that would define his career and legacy. In 1955, he hit .314 and collected 27 home runs and 106 RBIs. His performance got him to the All-Star Game. The following season was even better. He raised his average to .328, a National League-best.

In the 1957 season, Aaron flirted with a triple crown. He led in the home run and RBI categories, but his still-impressive .322 average was tied for third behind Stan Musial and Willie Mays. Aaron would get the last laugh, winning the MVP award and hitting a walk-off, pennant-clinching home run against Musial's Cardinals, the second-place team.

The 1957 Milwaukee Braves faced off in the World Series against the New York Yankees, the reigning champions. Aaron's World Series performance was crucial to his team securing the title. Throughout the seven-game series, Aaron batted .393, clubbing three home runs and seven RBIs.

The next year was almost like watching a rerun. Aaron's performance at the plate (.326 average, 30 home runs, and 95 RBIs) pushed the Braves to another pennant. They'd face the same New York Yankees in the World Series for the second year in a row. Unfortunately for Aaron and the Braves, the Yankees would be the victors this time.

Record-Breaking and Racism

While the Braves wouldn't reach the World Series again, Aaron continued to shine as one of the greatest players in the game. However, he was not always met with kind praise and handshakes. This was the 1950s and Black versus White tensions were still extremely high. Jackie Robinson may have broken baseball's color barrier, but it didn't mean every fan was happy about it, especially in southern states where Jim Crow-era rules were still on full display.

Growing up in Mobile, Alabama, Aaron dealt with racism from an early age. It was a time when it was sadly unavoidable. Even in his early baseball years, Aaron experienced vile and unfair treatment. In one account, he recalled eating at a restaurant in Washington D.C. while playing with the Negro League Indianapolis Clowns. After they finished their meal, the kitchen staff broke the plates the team used:

> What a horrible sound. Even as a kid, the irony of it hit me: here we were in the capital in the land of freedom and equality, and they had to destroy the plates that had touched the forks that had been in the mouths of black men. If dogs had eaten off those plates, they'd have washed them.

These types of experiences almost ended Aaron's career before it even began. With growing homesickness, Aaron told his family he was going to quit the minor leagues and return to Alabama. His brother, Herbert Aaron, convinced him otherwise and encouraged him to keep playing.

The unfair treatment continued during his time with the Jacksonville Braves. He had to make his own arrangements for food and housing, meaning he was often isolated from his teammates. If there was any silver lining to the racial abuse he faced, it was that it hardened his skin and prepared him, barely, for what was to come.

As years fell off the calendar, Aaron continued to build his career home run total. He was the eighth player in history to hit the 500 mark! A season later, there were only two players ahead of him for home run totals: Babe Ruth and Willie Mays. By 1971, his total was in the 600 range, and a year later he passed Mays. In the process, he broke Stan Musial's record for total bases in a career.

Edging closer to Ruth's record, and shattering other milestones from beloved (and predominately White) players, Aaron received so much mail the team had to hire a secretary to help him manage it. The US Postal Service gave him a plaque for receiving more mail than anyone aside from politicians. It was an honor that Aaron wished wasn't his because many of the letters were sent by hate-fueled racists, some threatening his life.

"Everybody loved Babe Ruth. You will be the most hated man in the country if you break his career home run record," read one. Another said, "You are doing more to hurt baseball than any other that ever played the game..." And a third: "I hope you join Brother Dr. Martin Luther King in that heaven, he spoke of."

These were the lightest of the remarks against Aaron, who would read every letter, good or bad, he received. "I had to know what I was up against," he said later. The worst examples of the hate mail are too vile to ever reprint again, even in the pursuit of telling Aaron's story.

The racist opponents of Aaron even went after the media when they praised or even simply covered Aaron's approach to Ruth's record. Lewis Grizzard, the acting executive sports editor for *The Atlanta Journal* received phone calls and letters so violent and threatening that he privately wrote an obituary for Hank Aaron, fearing the player would be murdered.

> *Sports Illustrated* took a direct take to the mountain of racism facing Aaron:

> Is this to be the year in which Aaron, at the age of thirty-nine, takes a moon walk above one of the most hallowed individual records in American Sports? Or will it be remembered as the season in which Aaron, the most dignified of athletes, was

besieged by hate mail and trapped by cobwebs and goblins that lurk in baseball's attic?

American cartoonist Charles Schulz, known for creating the *Peanuts* comic strips, also used pen and paper to take a stab at the deplorable behavior of some baseball fans. He ran a series of comics where the famous character Snoopy tries to break Babe Ruth's record, receiving hate mail in the process, always signed "a true baseball fan."

At the end of 1973, Aaron was one home run shy of Ruth's record. He'd have to wait until the 1974 campaign to take a crack at the Bambino's mark. With death threats increasing each day, Aaron (and many others) worried he wouldn't make it to the 1975 season.

Relief for the New Home Run King

The hate Hank Aaron experienced was not the majority sentiment. In a poll of baseball fans, 87% said they were on Aaron's side. He deserved recognition for his baseball talents and for beating Ruth's iconic record. Still, it's hard to pay attention to the positives when the remaining 13% represent people saying the opposite, especially when some population of that minority was sending death threats.

Aaron had another ally in attempting to quell the racist outcries surrounding his pursuit of Babe Ruth's home run record. The ally was Ruth's widow, Claire Hodgson.

Abhorred by the bigotry and public hatred surrounding Aaron's mounting home runs, she publicly stated that Babe Ruth would have only cheered on and supported Aaron's impressive hitting and propensity for home runs.

Aaron tied Ruth's record with the first swing of his bat for the 1974 season. Since the team was on the road, Braves management had attempted to bench Aaron to ensure the home run glory came at home in Atlanta where the team now called home. Bowie Kuhn, the acting MLB commissioner, required the Braves to play Aaron in at least two of the games. Luckily for Atlanta fans, he only hit one home run and returned home tied with Ruth's record.

On April 8, 1974, over 53,000 people showed up at the ballpark - but not to watch the Braves take on the visiting Dodgers. That was just a side note. They were there for a chance to see history being made and catch a glimpse of glory. The fanfare was on full display with a band playing before the game and a small arsenal of fireworks hidden just behind the outfield wall.

On his first trip to the plate, the crowd was on its feet cheering. If anyone in the crowd was against Aaron that day, their boos couldn't be heard. The only boos heard came when Aaron was walked on four pitches in the at-bat. The restless crowd didn't have to wait long for history. Aaron hit the record-breaking home run in the fourth inning, surpassing Ruth and creating pandemonium in the stadium. The crowd wouldn't quiet for another 11 minutes.

Legendary Vin Scully captured the moment and the significance perfectly:

> What a marvelous moment for baseball; what a marvelous moment for Atlanta and the State of George; what a marvelous moment for the country and the world. A black man is getting a standing ovation in the Deep South for breaking a record of an all-time baseball idol. And it is a great moment for all of us, and particularly for Henry Aaron.

For Aaron, it was just a relief. His iconic comments when asked how he felt after hitting the home run were simply, "Thank God it's over."

The Home Run Eclipse

The same day Hank Aaron hit a home run '715' to pass Babe Ruth in career home runs, he broke another record. When he walked in his first opportunity, teammate Dusty Baker came up and hit a ball into left field. Aaron read the play perfectly. He watched Bill Buckner misjudge the ball, giving him the chance to wheel around third base and score. It was his 2,063rd run, a new record previously held by Willie Mays.

It was a critical record to Aaron, perhaps more important than the home runs. Yet, none of the 53,000+ in attendance cared or even knew it happened. It was all about the home run, something Aaron would deal with for the rest of his life. "No matter what it is," Aaron said, "they're gonna always say, 'Hank Aaron and a home run."

Hank Aaron was not a home run hitter. That's a hard thing to say about a man who would end up hitting 755 of them in his career. But, it's the truth. Match him in a home run derby with Ruth, Bonds, Griffey Jr., Rodriguez, Mays, or any other player near his career record and he probably loses.

Aaron was more than a home run hitter. He was unequivocally the whole baseball player package. He was brilliant running the bases. He played the outfield with grace. He hit the ball hard and consistently. He was a pure hitter, not a home run hitter. The truth of the matter is when you hit the ball as hard and as consistently as Aaron, some of them will leave the yard. The problem is that everyone looks at home runs. It's the most dazzling offensive feat to most, meaning it distracts from everything else.

'Hank Aaron and a home run.'

In almost every year of his career, he led the league in some other offensive category, whether it was runs, total bases, average, doubles, hits, or another statistic. The home run record eclipses all of this. It eclipses arguably his best and most important record: total bases.

Aaron had 6,856 total bases in his career. The next closest player is Albert Pujols at 6,211. The gap between the two is startling. If Pujols wanted to catch Aaron, he'd need over 150 home runs. Pete Rose could have hit over 1,000 more singles and still been well shy of this record. If Stan Musial hit 350 more doubles, he wouldn't reach Aaron in total bases. And the Bambino, who Aaron is immortality linked to for home run hitting, would need more than 250 dingers to top the career total bases mark.

He did it all and did it longer than anyone else. It's his consistency and completeness that makes him not only one of the greatest hitters of all time but also one of the greatest players.

Did You Know?

- At 15 years old, Aaron participated in an MLB tryout for the Brooklyn Dodgers. He did not make the team.

- Hank Aaron holds an interesting record for most seasons hitting the same number of home runs as his uniform number. Aaron hit 44 home runs in four seasons. It's also interesting to note that when Aaron hit his record-breaking 715th home run, the pitcher's uniform was also #44.

- In his early days of playing, Aaron was given the nickname "Pork Chop" because he ordered it every time the team ate. "It was the only thing I knew to order off the menu," Aaron said.

- While he was professionally known as "Hank," he preferred to be called "Henry," his real name.

- Aaron was an avid fan of the NFL team the Cleveland Browns. He attended many games, disguising himself and sitting in the raucous "Dawg Pound" section of the stands.

- The address for the Atlanta Braves' current stadium, Truist Park, is 755 Battery Avenue. The '755' number is a nod to Aaron's career home run total.

CHAPTER 8:

BATTING TITLES, WARS, AND TED WILLIAMS

Williams never settled for being "good" at things. He always wanted to be perfect. If he couldn't do that, he'd get as close as possible. This persistence for greatness carried over into everything he did, from baseball to his hobbies to everyday conversation. "You'd see him one day and talk about some subject he didn't know," explained one of his business partners. "The next day, he'd bring up the same subject, and know more about it than you did."

He applied his inability and unwillingness to be average to every life pursuit, but nothing more than baseball. To outsiders, it would appear that everything came easily to Williams. This was part of his allure - making difficult things look easy.

Yet, it wasn't always natural talent. He worked hard, watched carefully, analyzed relentlessly, and studied always. He trained the two most important parts of his body: his eyes and his brain. With these two organs operating at peak efficiency, he could use his broad, 6'3" frame to complete incredible feats, whether on the baseball diamond or in the sky.

Williams at the Plate

Every baseball player, at many points in their career, aspires to be the greatest ever. It's a backyard or sandlot dream for most. Reality sets in for most players, even most major leaguers. 'I'm good, but I'm not *that* good.' Ted Williams never had this internal dialog. And, if he did, he didn't listen to that nagging voice in his head. Williams always aspired to be the best ever.

"A man has to have goals, for a day, for a lifetime, and that was mine, to have people say, 'There goes Ted Williams, the greatest hitter who ever lived,'" said Williams. He was fanatical in his pursuit of this goal. He watched everything everyone did when it came to hitting, including opposing pitchers. His careful eyes and analytical brain would figure out a pitcher's plan. Williams knew what pitch was coming before the pitcher did.

Bobby Shantz best sums up the pitcher's perspective with Williams standing at the plate. "Did they tell me how to pitch to [Williams?] Sure, they did. It was great advice, and very encouraging. They said he had no weakness, won't swing at a bad ball, has the best eyes in the business and can kill you with one swing. He won't hit anything bad, but don't give him anything good."

On the rare occasion a pitcher struck him out, Williams was known to find the player after (or during) the game and demand to know what he threw, why he threw it, how hard he threw it, etc. He had the same approach to his fellow hitters, always asking for others to divulge their batting secrets. If a player had a weird stance or grip, Williams had to know why.

Today, players have all the intel they need thanks to analytics and detailed scouting. Williams did the number-crunching analytics in his head, on the fly. He looked for advantages and improvements wherever he could, from his bats, diet, stance, etc. "[Williams] studied hitting the way a broker studies the stock market, and could spot at a glance, mistakes that others couldn't see in a week," explained Carl Yastrzemski, another Red Sox legend.

The crown jewel of Williams' career is the season he batted .406 (more on this later), but that achievement makes it easy to overlook everything else Williams did. Those well-trained eyes were infallible at the plate. Williams is the career leader for on-base percentage. He also ranks fourth all-time for walks, trailing behind Barry Bonds, Rickey Henderson, and Babe Ruth.

However, Williams had fewer years and plate appearances, giving the other names on the list an advantage. He walked more often (about once every 4.85 appearances) than the others, even Bonds (one walk per 4.93 appearances). More impressive is Williams' ratio of walks to strikeouts. Babe Ruth had 41 more walks than Williams, but struck out 621 more times, too.

Williams struck out in only 7% of his plate appearances. Bonds, Henderson, and Ruth struck out over 12% of their PAs.

If the term "hitter" is applied literally, meaning someone who hits the ball and reaches base safely, Williams is in the conversation for greatest ever next to Honus Wagner, Ty Cobb, and the like. When it comes to being the greatest *batter of all time,* Williams is the conversation. He reached base at a higher rate than anyone else, rarely made mistakes at the plate, and did it consistently and despite interruptions to his baseball career to serve the country.

Williams in the Sky

Shortly after the famous 1941 season when Williams batted .406 on the year, the Japanese surprise-attacked Pearl Harbor, prompting the US to enter World War II. Ted Williams would enlist in the Navy, putting his occupation as a baseball star on hold. Williams' fine-tuned brain, eyes, reflexes, and athleticism now focused on becoming a pilot.

Johnny Pesky entered pilot training with Williams. He quickly became frustrated at his teammate's natural talent. While Pesky would spend hours studying and making sense of navigational charts, he'd still struggle during the frequent tests. Williams, on the other hand, studied less (sometimes not at all) and scored better. "I could fly the plane; I just had no idea where I was going," Pesky explained.

Williams would finish his aviation training ahead of schedule. His aptitude for flying was obvious to superior officers. He would stay at the advanced pilot training site in Pensacola, Florida, to train the next round of incoming pilots. (Pesky wouldn't make it to advanced training). At the end of World War II, Williams was stationed at Pearl Harbor, waiting for orders to enter the Pacific Ocean theater of battle. He never saw combat and returned to Boston safely.

While Williams was officially released from service, he remained active in the Marine Corps Reserve. This status brought him back to armed conflict during the Korean War in 1952. He was given the opportunity for an easy enlistment playing baseball with other servicemen. He turned the safer job down and went back to piloting.

Flying in the Korean War was much different. The military had replaced its propeller crafts with jet fighters. Williams had to relearn most of the controls. As always, Williams made it look easy. He was back to flying in no time, often as a wingman for John Glenn, a future astronaut. Glenn considered Williams one of the best pilots he'd seen, which speaks to the baseball player's excellence in his military career. In total, he participated in almost 40 combat missions.

Approaching Perfection

"Baseball is the only field of endeavor where a man can succeed three times out of ten and be considered a good performer," Ted Williams famously said. This is a common concept in baseball. A .300 hitter in a season is a top performer, likely an all-star. If that hitter repeats this success over their career, they'll be in the Hall of Fame.

Williams knew real perfection in baseball was impossible; everyone is going to swing and miss eventually. Yet, being a "good performer," in his own words, wasn't enough. He strived to be as close to perfect as his skills permitted. If he couldn't be perfect, he'd at least become the best.

In 1941, Williams ended the season with a .406 average. It was the highest season average since Roger Hornsby hit .424 in 1924. Since then, no one has hit the magic .400 mark. A few players came close, even getting within a handful of hits to reach this rarefied air. George Brett needed only five more hits in 1980 to push his .390 average with the extra points needed.

Yet, aside from a few close calls, it's been over 80 years, and no one has hit the mark. As more years go by, Williams and his .406 season become more folkloric and legendary. "If I had known hitting .400 was going to be such a big deal, I would have done it again," Williams joked later in life.

The mythic status of the .400 mark grows each year because, despite state-of-the-art training and advanced analytics, hitting has gotten harder. Through the last 10 years, the top batting average for the season was roughly .342. In 2022, Jeff McNeil led the majors with a batting average of .3265. It was the lowest season-best average since 1963 (Tommy Davis led with .3255).

In the same 10 recent seasons, only two players have hit above .350. Go back 20 seasons and the number edges up slightly to include eight more names. The 2000 season alone had five batters hitting above the .350 mark.

The bottom line is hitting is incredibly hard, and getting more challenging by the year. When you look at hitters today, Williams' .406 mark seems firmly set in the stratosphere - untouchable, eternal, and perfect.

Did You Know?

- During military training, Williams stepped into a boxing ring with a former pro fighter who noticed the baseball players' fast reflexes. After sparring, the instructor asked Williams if he'd like to "make a fast million dollars," saying he could train him as a boxer. There truly was nothing he wasn't great at.

- Ted Williams' body and head are frozen separately in liquid nitrogen at the Alcor Life Extension Foundation in Scottsdale, Arizona.

- Outside of baseball, Williams had many hobbies and interests. Most notably, he loved to fish and hunt. He did both all over the world. He retired in Islamorada, Florida because of the superb fishing spots.

- When Williams entered the Hall of Fame in 1966, he used the platform to speak out for the Negro League stars. "I hope that someday the names of Satchel Paige and Josh Gibson in some way can be added to the symbol of the great Negro League players that are not here only because they were not given a chance." Five years later, Satchel Paige entered the Hall of Fame.

- Ted Williams was known for being picky about his bats. In 1948, he received a letter from 14-year-old David

Pressman. The young fan told Williams he should dry his bats every day because the wood absorbs moisture, adding as much as three ounces to the weight. Williams adopted the practice and continued it for the remainder of his career.

- Similar to Babe Ruth, Williams also had a long list of nicknames, including "the Splendid Splinter," "the Kid," "Thumper," and "Teddy Ballgame."

CHAPTER 9:

SANDY KOUFAX, THE LEFT ARM OF GOD

Sandy Koufax is in a rare air of baseball players. No matter who enters the game or how their stats compare, some fans will always regard Koufax as the greatest ever. The reasons don't matter. He's just one of those players; he's 'the guy' in many people's heads.

Buzzie Bavasi was a GM for the Dodgers. He tells a story about his collection of 22 signed baseballs of various players from his days as a manager. He kept the balls in the study of his home in California. The autographed balls included names like DiMaggio, Musial, Mays, Aaron, and more. "Somebody broke in here," Bavasi says in Jane Leavy's Sandy Koufax biography. "What do you think they took? One ball. Sandy's. I never laughed so much in my life."

Why just the Koufax ball?

Part of Koufax's eternal appeal is his exit from the game. Koufax retired in 1966 at the young age of 30. His stats the season before hardly paint a picture of a declining player past his prime. In fact, it was arguably his best season yet. He won the Cy Young unanimously, collecting 27 wins, including five shutouts. He struck out 317 batters during the 1966 season and had a 1.73 ERA. He was untouchable.

Koufax's decision to retire at the top of the game and so young was a shock to everyone. It's contrary to what's expected of baseball players and athletes in general. You love the game as much as the fans. Thus, you play the game as long as your body allows. That's the rule, right? Koufax never bought it. In emancipating himself from this expectation, he left the game entirely on his own terms and entirely untarnished.

His departure from the game was like John Wayne riding off into the sunset in one of his 80-something cowboy movies, Koufax disappeared from baseball almost entirely. Rarely was he seen or heard from again.

He cut ties from baseball so entirely and so young that people perpetually wondered what he did all day. What was his plan for a second act? If time machines were real and anyone had the chance to go back to 1966 to ask Koufax, he'd likely say he didn't have one. Rather, he was simply intent on having a chapter outside of baseball.

Dusty Baker was the closest anyone got to an actual answer to Koufax's plan. "He said he's gonna just be a farmer someplace, have very few clothes on and ride a tractor around all day." The short answer: he was going to enjoy his life.

Koufax wasn't going to cash in on his fame like many other players (at least not until the money dried up). No post-retirement endorsements or public appearance tours. He just left. In doing so, he preserved his legacy. People remembered him exactly how he was because for years there was no other Sandy. Baseball Koufax and present-day

Koufax are different not because of age or baseball capability, but because he designed it that way.

The Wind-Up and the Pitch

One of the enchanting qualities of Sandy Koufax was his wind-up. While many fans would refer to it as poetry in motion, there was nothing artful about it. It was science. Koufax understood the human body as a mechanism. "Everybody who performs an athletic event of any kind is a system of levers," he said. He treated his pitching delivery like a catapult. If leverage, weight, and energy are used properly, you don't need muscular force.

Over his career, Koufax perfected being a catapult. He could repeat his motions with the same consistency as the medieval weaponry he designed himself after. Years later, Dr. Marilyn Pink, a biomechanical researcher analyzed his pitching motion. "There was absolutely not a wasted piece of energy there. He knew exactly what was extraneous and what was needed," reported Dr. Pink.

The result of this biomechanical perfection has been captured time and time again by the batters he faced.

> **Willie Stargell:** "Somebody asked me one time, 'What's it like hitting off of Koufax?' I said, you ever drink coffee with a fork?"

103

Andy Etchebarren: "With Koufax, your eyes couldn't tell your brain to react in time."

Willie Mays: "I knew every pitch he was going to throw, fastball, breaking ball or whatever. Actually, he would let you look at it. And you still couldn't hit it."

Ron Santo: "This guy (Koufax) could drive you to drink."

Don Sutton: "A foul ball off of Koufax was a moral victory."

Allan Roth: "When anybody got a hit off him, people would turn to each other and say, 'Gee, I wonder what he did wrong.'

Casey Stengel: "Umpires often can't see where Koufax pitches go, so they have to judge from the sound of the ball hitting the catcher's glove."

Pee Wee Reese: "I never saw anybody throw that hard in my life, and I've faced some of the greatest in the game."

And then there was his fastball. Expert physicists have long debunked the idea of a rising fastball. You would have to throw inhumanely fast with ample backspin to create the necessary lift for the ball to theoretically rise. Remember, pitchers, are throwing a weighted ball at a downward angle due to the height of the mound.

Simply put, a rising pitch defies gravity. Hitters who claim to have faced a rising fastball are, according to aforementioned expert physicists, experiencing an optical illusion. The ball is moving faster than the eyes and brain can accurately process. Batters aren't seeing the entire path of the ball but snapshots, like a cartoon flipbook. The eyes and brain *think* the ball is rising because it isn't dropping as expected.

Yet, there are many hitters who, when it comes to Koufax's fastball, say physics and gravity be damned.

> **Willie Mays:** "I don't know how much it rose; it just rose."
>
> **Carl Erksine:** "It accelerated. It came again."
>
> **Dave Wallace:** "Where the grass ends and the dirt begins, it got an afterburner."
>
> **Al Campanis:** "There are two times in my life the hair on my arms has stood up: the first time I saw the ceiling of the Sistine Chapel and the second time I saw Sandy Koufax throw a fastball."

There are similar accounts of disbelief regarding the second pitch in Koufax's arsenal, his curveball. It had the kind of 12-to-6 drop that made seasoned hitters swing and miss by comical margins. To call it a curveball is like calling a lion a cat; it may be technically correct but that doesn't make it right. The pitch even fooled some catchers who knew what pitch was coming. They'd start to stand to catch what they thought was a high fastball, thinking, "Maybe Sandy got the signs mixed up?" Then, the catcher would feel the ball strike them in the leg guards.

The lack of technology in Koufax's time adds to the mystic nature of his pitching. With no radar guns, advanced analytics, instant replay, or the like, only blurry video footage and the accounts of players, like those mentioned above, capture his dominance.

The Swing and the Miss

All of the sentiments about Koufax and his pitches would indicate a player as perfect as his windup. That version of Koufax didn't exist yet. He was young and still finding himself as a pitcher. In his first appearance on a major league mound, he let up a bloop single, threw away a ball bunted back to him, and then walked Hank Aaron on four pitches.

His next appearance marked his first official major league start. He walked eight batters in under five full innings. He didn't start another game for nearly two weeks. This was a repeating theme. Koufax had two things working against him. The first was his untamed control which made even teammates unwilling to stand in the box to give him practice.

The second was a manager, Walter Alston, on a one-year contract that didn't want to ruin his chances of an extension by taking risks, like utilizing a young and unproven pitcher. The opportunities Koufax did get were short. Dick Young of the *Daily News* describes how a typical Koufax appearance went:

> Alston manifests very little confidence in Koufax...Koufax started in St. Louis the other night. He was leading, 3-1, in the fourth, when he walked the leadoff man and threw two balls to the next hitter. Carl Erskine, who had been warming up since the first inning, was relieved.

This was largely how it went for the first five seasons. Even when Koufax found his form and felt he had a place in the starting rotation, he was inexplicably sat for extended periods. He asked to be traded to a team that would use him, but it never happened. At the conclusion of the 1960 season, he was ready to give baseball up entirely.

Koufax arrived at the 1961 spring training camp in revived form. He had spent the winter working out, determined to see how good he could be at pitching before he left the game. Koufax received valuable advice on his pitching motion and approach during the camp. It proved to be the input he needed. He posted record-breaking numbers that year, including an NL-best 269 strikeouts.

The 1962 season continued Koufax's success. At the new Dodger Stadium, his ERA dropped from 4.29 to 1.75. He also threw a no-hitter that included an immaculate inning (three strikeouts on nine pitches). Koufax threw another no-hitter the next season, benefiting greatly from an expanded strike zone. He won the NL MVP, World Series MVP, and Cy Young Award in the same year.

Koufax pitched a third no-hitter in 1964 and led the league with a 1.74 ERA. However, in April and August, he had two incidents of soreness in his pitching arm and elbow. By 1965, the issues in his arm were worse. Koufax needed oils before the game, pain medicine during, and an ice bath for his arm after. The team physician warned him that too much use could result in loss of feeling.

Despite the warnings, Koufax pitched more innings than any player that year. He also led in wins, ERA, and strikeouts. His 382 strikeouts were a record at the time, later topped by Nolan Ryan (383). He was an obvious and unanimous pick for the Cy Young Award. It was also the fourth year in a row he pitched a no-hitter. This time, his no-hitter doubled as Koufax's first and only perfect game. The Dodgers won the Series yet again, thriving behind Koufax's dominant pitching.

The Dodgers would also reach the World Series the following season but were swept in four games by the Baltimore Orioles. Koufax pitched well, despite still struggling with pain in his elbow, but didn't receive support from the Dodgers' bats. After that 1966 season, Koufax announced his retirement, no longer willing to pitch with his arthritic elbow.

That was that. The 30-year-old star, the most dominant pitcher of the time, rode off into the sunset, leaving baseball at the peak of success.

Did You Know?

- Sandy Koufax pitched a perfect game on September 9, 1965. It was his fourth no-hitter (a record at the time that was later broken by Nolan Ryan). The opposing pitcher, Bob Hendley, gave up only one hit and an unearned run. The game holds the record for the fewest combined hits.

- As a youth, Koufax loved basketball more than baseball. He could have made a career out of it, too. In a marketing ploy in 1953, the New York Knicks played scrimmage matches with local high schools. When they visited Lafayette High School, a young Koufax took the court opposite the Knicks. Harry "the Horse" Gallatin of the Knicks was so impressed by the high schooler he told Koufax's coach, "We'll be coming back for this kid some day."

- Retiring early from his career allowed Koufax to become the youngest Hall of Fame inductee. He was just 36 years old. The next youngest is Roberto Clemente who was specially inducted after his early death. Clemente was 38.

- Sandy Koufax was actually born Sanford Braun. His parents divorced and Sandy took the name of his mother's new husband, Irving Koufax.

- Aside from the then-Brooklyn Dodgers, Koufax also received offers to play for the Pittsburgh Pirates and Milwaukee Braves. The Braves and Pirates even offered more money. However, Koufax and his father had already made a hand-shake deal with the Dodgers that they refused to go back on, demonstrating the integrity of Koufax.

- Koufax pitched the final inning of the 1957 season. The Brooklyn Dodgers made their cross-country move to Los Angeles prior to the 1958 season, making Koufax the last person to pitch for the Brooklyn Dodgers.

CHAPTER 10:

CAL RIPKEN JR. BECOMES IRON MAN

Baseball players are often treated like machines. If you want to play third base at the major league level, the expectation is you can make the throw across the diamond to first base 100% of the time. If you can't do that, you better do it 99.99% of the time. If you bat .300, you're a successful hitter with a job. Hit much more than that and you're an All-Star. Less and you become replaceable.

It's the only sport with the Error statistic—a measure of inefficient machines making mistakes. Scoreboards post these mistakes in glowing numbers to remind the errored machine of their miscalculation for the remainder of the game.

Of course, machines also break down. They need repairs. How long it takes a machine to return to working order is all the time they aren't performing their functions. Some machines are so finely tuned, repairs are never needed. The Centennial Light Bulb, for instance, has been on for well over 100 years, only turning off during power failures and outages.

Cal Ripken Jr. was the closest thing the baseball world has ever seen to an unbreakable machine. He played in 2,632 consecutive games, breaking a record set by Lou Gehrig decades before. Even after setting the record, Ripken Jr. chugged on for over 502 games.

More miraculous and worthy of the title of baseball's best machine was how many consecutive *innings* he played:

113

8,243. That's 904 complete, consecutive games. When you consider that baseball players in Ripken Jr.'s time squeezed 162 games into only 183 days, baseball's Iron Man had 0.8 days off a week, equaling roughly three days out of the month. He was more reliable than the US Postal Service and its 'nor rain, nor snow' motto.

Becoming Iron Man

Cal Ripken Jr.'s constitution was tested early in his career before any talks of consecutive game streaks. It was during his time with the Triple-A Rochester Red Wings. His team, facing the Pawtucket Red Sox, played the longest professional baseball game in history.

The game lasted 33 innings and took over eight hours to finish. Most of the game - 32 out of 33 innings - was played in one day, late into the night. Finally, the teams agreed to postpone the remainder of the game for another day. Ripken had 15 plate appearances, a record he shares with two teammates.

Two months after the 33-inning saga, Ripken made his debut in the majors with the Baltimore Orioles. The next season (1982), he claimed the Rookie of the Year title, quickly establishing himself as one of the best defensive and offensive stars in the game. It was during this rookie year that 21-year-old Ripken sat out a game during a doubleheader. By the time he'd miss his next game, he would be a 38-year-old veteran.

The first test of Ripken's consecutive streak came early on. During the start of the 1985 season, he sprained his ankle. Despite the injury, he stayed in the game. More impressively, he played the following game two days later. It was the first showcase of Cal Ripken Jr. the Iron Man. Whether injured or not, Ripken was ready to play.

In 1987, Ripken's father, Cal Ripken Sr., took the manager job for the Orioles, creating a unique father-son dynamic on the team. It was the same year Cal Jr.'s consecutive innings streak ended, sitting mid-game at the request of his father-manager. Sadly, the family reunion didn't last long. Ripken Sr. left the coaching position the following season.

By 1991, Cal Ripken Jr.'s streak was second only to Lou Gehrig. Ripken wasn't just showing up to games; he was thriving on the diamond and in the batter's box. He won the AL MVP, All-Star Game MVP, Gold Glove for shortstop, and won the 1991 Home Run Derby; all in 1991.

The following season tested Ripken's grit again. After a bench-clearing brawl with the Seattle Mariners, Ripken felt soreness in his knee and doubted his participation in the next game. When the knee felt better by game time, he changed his mind and took the field. Ripken's batting started slumping, bringing into question his lack of rest.

The Oriole coach defended the player, reiterating that only Ripken could tell when he needed a day off.

He corrected his slumping batting and the consecutive game streak continued. On September 6, 1995, Ripken passed Gehrig's record in front of a packed crowd at Camden Yards. When the record became official in the fifth inning, there was a 22-minute pause as baseball's new Iron Man received a standing ovation and took a lap around the stadium.

"Tonight, I stand here, overwhelmed, as my name is linked with the great and courageous Lou Gehrig," Ripken, respectful as ever, remarked in his speech. "I'm truly humbled to have our names spoken in the same breath." Ripken's streak continued for 502 more games before he ended it on his own terms.

A Record As Ironclad As The Man Himself

Some records in baseball fall outside conventional wisdom. Not all records are meant to be broken. Due to various circumstances and changes to the game throughout history, some records are untouchable. Cal Ripken Jr.'s record of 2,632 consecutive games played will never be broken.

Today's players rest more often to protect against injuries. Even a healthy player will get scheduled days off.

After all, even machines need rest in a 162-game season! These days off allow players to rest and recover from everyday soreness, reducing the risk of both minor and major injuries.

So, a Cal Ripken Jr. playing today would likely sit out games from time to time, whether he wanted to or not. It's just a different game. However, that's not a good reason to explain why the consecutive game record will not be broken. It greatly undermines Ripken's achievement.

In any era and at any time, playing 2,632 consecutive games is practically inhuman. Ripken is the embodiment of the saying, "showing up is half the battle." He showed up and played more consecutive games than anyone else, by a significant margin. He could have passed Gehrig and then taken a day off. Instead, he kept showing up for 502 more games.

The margin between Ripken and Gehrig is significant, but it's nothing compared to the gap between the Baltimore shortstop and the other names on the consecutive games played list. Everett Scott had a streak between 1916 and 1925 that lasted 1,307 games. He's third on the all-time streak list. Steve Garvey had another great run, taking the fourth all-time spot with a 1207-game streak in the 70s and 80s. If you combine both, it's still over 100 consecutive games shy of Ripken.

It's an impossible record to break because of everything that needs to fall in place for it to happen. It isn't a conversation about if it will ever be broken, or who could pass Ripken. The real puzzle is *how* someone breaks it. It may be a question that only the man himself can answer.

Did You Know?

- Cal Ripken Jr.'s first appearance in Major League Baseball was as a pinch-runner in a game against the Kansas City Royals. Ripken would end up scoring the winning run.

- The most recent consecutive game streak was set by Whit Merrifield. It began on June 24, 2018, and ended on July 11, 2022, lasting 553 games.

- Kirby Puckett, Don Mattingly, Lenny Dykstra, Cecil Fielder, and many other notable stars played their entire careers within Ripken Jr.'s streak.

- Cal Ripken Jr. gets a lot of attention for his consecutive game record and defensive skills. However, he also holds the record for the most home runs by a shortstop, speaking to his skills at the plate.

- In 1987, Cal Ripken Sr. managed both his sons, Cal Jr. and Billy, on the Orioles.

- Ripken Jr. also holds the international record for consecutive games played. After toppling Gehrig's record of 2130 games, Ripken went on to pass Sachio Kinugasa, who played 2,215 consecutive games in Japan.

CHAPTER 11:

JIM ABBOTT PROVES EVERYONE WRONG

Baseball is an incredibly difficult sport to play. Two or three-sport athletes frequently declare baseball the hardest of the group. "That ball does some things to you," said NFL *and* MLB star Deion Sanders. "That's a hard sport." It's also the hardest sport to play at the highest level.

The MLB draft is the longest by a wide margin. Even with new standards to reduce it to 20 rounds (more than half what it used to be), it's still nearly three times longer than the NFL draft and 10 times longer than the NFL or NBA. This creates a massive pool of incoming players flooding minor league rosters each year, meaning it is something of a statistical nightmare for any player to achieve their MLB debut.

In one study, the odds of making it to the MLB were just 0.17%. That's less than your odds of being hit by lightning. Even players drafted in the first round are not guaranteed an MLB roster spot, not even close. First-rounders have a 9.6% odds of making it to the majors. These are players teams expect will be future stars and over 90% of the time they don't get it right!

It doesn't paint a promising picture. Now, imagine you're Jim Abbott attempting to overcome these odds and become a player in the big leagues. From day one, you have a startling disadvantage compared to every other player in the draft pool - you were born with only one hand.

Standing Out for the Wrong Reasons

From a young age, Abbott had to rely largely on himself for encouragement. Getting bullied or excluded by peers is something every child fears and experiences. Abbott's missing hand made him the target of both at unimaginable levels. Stories from his childhood are heartbreaking.

Some classmates would make jokes or hurtful comments. Others would stay away from him altogether because his disability scared or upset them. A prosthetic hand only made it worse. And, there were plenty of activities, even simple things like tying shoes, which Abbott struggled to perform with just one hand. His mother would tie his shoes as tight as possible in the morning, hoping they wouldn't come undone and leave Abbott an easy target for more jeers from classmates.

His parents were his biggest supporters, along with a third-grade teacher who would take time out of his day to teach Abbott a method for tying shoes one-handed, saving him future torment from classmates. When the future MLB-er wanted to try sports, his parents backed him fully, offering help when they could. "But in the end," his father says, "It was all Jim. It had to be."

Abbott practiced relentlessly, finding techniques to play baseball without a second hand. He was dominant from a young age, even throwing a no-hitter in one of his first

Little League games. Yet, despite his successes, the responses always included a sense of doubt. He would continuously face people demanding he set more realistic goals than being a professional baseball pitcher. Even when he was the most dominant player on a team, players and coaches would doubt his capabilities.

"You won't be this good next year with the older boys." Or, "How long do you really think you'll stay competitive?" If Abbott dared to share his dream of becoming a pitcher in Major League Baseball, the responses were even more dismissive. "There are thousands of two-handed people trying to make the big leagues. Why would any team take a player with only one hand?"

The criticism and doubt were constant, but Abbott never lost sight of his goal. He continued to excel at every level of play. His high school coach liked his pitching but couldn't see him fielding or hitting. Yet, Abbott did both of these exceptionally well. In his senior year, he hit seven home runs and batted .427, better than most of his two-handed teammates. On the mound, his stats were even more eye-catching. He had an ERA of 0.76 and an incredible average strikeout rate of two per inning.

A Worldwide Talent

Abbott's high school stats enticed the Toronto Blue Jays to select him in the 1985 MLB draft. Even though he was picked in the final round, he would have received a $50,000 bonus. Plus, he'd have the opportunity to pursue his dream and prove the naysayers wrong once and for all. Wisely, Abbott declined the offer and attended college at the University of Michigan instead. He wanted to continue honing his baseball talents and, hopefully, receive an even better MLB offer in the future.

With the Michigan Wolverines, Abbott quickly added to the already long list of baseball achievements. During his time at the University of Michigan, the baseball team won two conference championships. Abbott pitched a no-hitter in the NCAA tournament in his sophomore year and had an 11-3 record on the season.

The same year of his tournament no-hitter, Abbott participated in the Pan-American games, bringing his talents and an incredible story to the worldwide stage. He was given the honor to wave the American flag during the opening ceremonies. Team USA, backed by his phenomenal pitching talents, would come home with a silver medal. A year later, he was on a different Team USA, this time competing in the 1988 Olympics in Seoul, South Korea.

Again, his talents shone. He got the ball in the final game against Japan and pitched a complete game win.

The worldwide stage proved Abbott could play at the highest levels. However, his successes were often outshined by the media's attention to his disability. It was never a story about Jim Abbott, the incredible pitcher. It was always the story of Jim Abbott, the one-handed pitcher. It wasn't the attention the young player wanted. Everyone seemed to care about the one thing Abbott wanted to ignore.

Nonetheless, the international attention and growing pile of awards and accolades gave Abbott the MLB-quality resume he needed. He opted out of his final year at the University of Michigan and entered the 1988 MLB draft. This time, he would not be taken in the last round. The California Angels drafted him in the first round with the eighth overall pick. His signing bonus was $207,000.

His position in the draft and comfy signing bonus sent a clear message. The Angels thought he was a top talent and worthy of a substantial financial investment. It was one of the rare moments where the only thing that mattered was his pitching chops.

Big League Career

Jim Abbott's MLB career spanned 10 years and would see him in four different team uniforms. While most players spend time in the minors to mature and build on their existing skills, Abbott skipped this phase. His professional baseball debut was at the major league level. He was only the 15th player since the draft started in 1965 to go straight to the big leagues.

This was not something handed to Abbott. It wasn't a PR move to generate buzz around the Angels for selecting a player with a disability. He earned his spot on the MLB roster with hard work and exceptional performance during the spring. Every time he took the mound during preseason games, he dominated, even against top MLB talents.

The story of the one-handed pitcher making his MLB debut made headlines everywhere. His first game was widely televised, even in other countries. While his initial outing wasn't a successful one (he'd lose the game and pitch only a few innings), he received a standing ovation when left the field. *Baseball America* ranked his debut second in history behind Jackie Robinson.

The applause wasn't what Abbott wanted to hear. He likely didn't even hear it. His attention was on fixing his mistakes and getting wins. That first win would come against the Baltimore Orioles. From there, his rookie season was relatively smooth sailing. He'd finish the year 12-12 with a 3.92 ERA. It was a solid performance. It was the second most wins by a first-year pitcher. He was even in the running for Rookie of the Year, landing fifth in the voting.

The 1991 season was arguably Abbott's best. He came close to winning the 'Cy Young Award'. He had a winning 18-11 record and a 2.89 ERA. His earned run average improved the next year to 2.77, but he failed to maintain a positive win-loss ratio. Wins and losses aside, Abbott had established himself as a successful, top-level pitcher. The New York Yankees thought so, too. They traded for him in late 1992 in exchange for three players.

His numbers with the Bronx Bombers never reached the same heights as his time with the Angels. Part of this was due to a difficult salary arbitration process with the Yankees. The New York organization cited several reasons to reject his request for $3.5M. The negative sentiments wore on Abbott. Why trade for a pitcher if your opinions of him are so low?

Stats and hurt feelings aside, he's fondly remembered in pinstripes because of a no-hitter against Cleveland in 1993. The win galvanized the Yankees amid a tough pennant race. Unfortunately, the impact of his tremendous hitless game didn't last. By the end of the year, the Yankees fell out of convention and ended the season in second place, seven games behind Toronto.

A Good Pitcher

The difficult part of discussing Jim Abbott's legacy is it is always tied to the elephant in the room - his missing hand. It eclipses his achievements like the home run record does for Hank Aaron. Yet, for someone who spent his entire life trying to get people to forget about his physical handicap, it's not how Abbott wants people to remember his career. He likely wouldn't even agree to calling it a handicap.

His numbers in most seasons were good, but maybe not great. Sometimes, they were below average. But, there's always the caveat that he did it with one hand, which changes how sports people define good, great, and bad years. That doesn't sit right with Abbott. "I'll always be looked at as having played with one hand," he admitted. "How other people see it is up to them. The only thing that matters to me is a sense of giving everything I've got and making the most of what I've been given.

Abbott is the first to admit he wasn't destined for the Hall of Fame. After his no-hitter with the Yankees, there were few bright spots left in his career. He even retired briefly after the 1996 season, his worst year yet (a 2-18 record with a 7.48 ERA). Upon returning, he had a few good starts. Abbott always seemed like a guy about to make a comeback, but it never happened.

That's how it goes for a lot of baseball players, especially pitchers. You can be dominant for two years and mediocre for eight. There are plenty of factors that can weaken a pitcher's effectiveness, Injuries happen, batters start seeing pitches better, velocity decreases, etc. Abbott was no exception.

At the end of Abbott's career, there was plenty to applaud. He threw a no-hitter and almost pitched himself to a Cy Young. He competed internationally and brought home a Gold Medal for Team USA. That's the Jim Abbott story. Everything else is a minor detail.

Did You Know?

- In 1987, Jim Abbott received the Golden Spikes Award, given to the top amateur baseball player. Other names in the running included Ken Griffey Jr., Robin Ventura, and Jack McDowell.

- Abbott was the first baseball player to receive the Sullivan Award, recognizing the best amateur athlete in the country.

- The University of Michigan retired his #31 uniform in 1999. He is also in the Athletic Hall of Honor.

- Abbott is a member of the College Baseball Hall of Fame and Michigan Sports Hall of Fame.

- Worried he may be tipping pitches, the New York Yankees invented a special glove for Abbott, but he didn't find it comfortable and never used it during a game.

- Today, Abbott does public speaking tours, inspiring future generations to pursue their goals despite disabilities and other challenges.

CHAPTER 12:

THE ONE-ARMED PETE GRAY

Jim Abbott was often compared to another player named Pete Gray. The two shared similar handicaps; Pete Gray had lost his arm in an accident as a child. Abbott hated the comparisons. Gray wasn't even a pitcher! "I wanted to be like Nolan Ryan," said Abbott. "I didn't want to be like Pete Gray." The only real similarity between these two players is their inspirational drive to play baseball at the highest level, especially in the face of adversity and doubt.

Gray (was born as Peter J. Wyshner) had baseball dreams before the accident that claimed his right arm when he was very young. "I can't remember when I haven't had the ambition to be a ballplayer," he said. As a natural righty, he now had to train himself to throw with his left.

He also had to invent a means to catch and field with one arm. For his method to work, he had to remove the padding from his glove. This made it easier to tuck the glove under his arm to transfer it to his hand and make the throw. Unfortunately, removing the padding, left his hand more vulnerable to stingers.

It would have been easy to find a new passion, but Gray wasn't the type. He played baseball whenever and wherever he could. Of course, he was immune to blending in, drawing sympathy or jeers for his disability. He didn't want either. Similar to Abbott, he never wanted to be treated differently because of his amputated arm. He just wanted to play baseball.

Persistence

No one aside from Gray had faith in his dream. He was relentless in trying out for teams and trying to display his talents to coaches and players. Most people didn't give him the time of day. When he approached the last-place Athletics, Manager Connie Mack told him, "Son, I've got men with two arms who can't play this game."

That was a polite response compared to others. Not everyone was as patient. For instance, Doc Prothro shouted, "Get off the field, Wingy!" after Gray tried to participate in the Phillies' training camp.

Unable to find any team or coach willing to take a chance on him, he decided to try a more persuasive tactic. He approached a semi-pro team's owner with a $10 bill. Gray told him he could keep it if he didn't impress on the field. The owner accepted, allowing the one-armed player to participate in the game. He hit a home run in this first game, earning a spot on the team. (It's unclear if the owner ever returned the $10).

Gray's talents on the diamond quickly won his new teammates over. He was speedy on the basepaths, grabbing extra bases when he could. His one-handed batting technique was also a marvel. He even had the power in his arm to hit home runs. By this point, Gray had become so adept at his unconventional fielding method, there was hardly any delay. Players soon forgot he was missing an arm at all.

"I was sure when I came here this guy (Gray) wasn't going to be with us long," remarked one of his teammates. "Now, I'm not so sure...I see him doing things out there I didn't think he could." Gray was named MVP during one season of semi-pro baseball. However, he was still in pursuit of his bigger dream: to play in the big leagues.

Opportunity

Baseball in the 1940s was an interesting time. With the world fighting a war in Europe, professional baseball nearly collapsed. Many of the game's best hitters were serving overseas. The list includes players like Hank Greenberg, Ted Williams, Joe DiMaggio, Bob Feller, Stan Musial, and Warren Spahn. That's an incomplete list of *only* future Hall of Famers. There were plenty of good-not-great players that also put down their bats to pick up rifles.

The war left gaping holes in every team, putting owners in precarious situations. There were talks of baseball pausing or ending altogether. This may have happened had it not been for President Franklin D. Roosevelt issuing his famous letter requesting baseball to continue.

To allow baseball to persist, teams needed to fix the holes in their rosters. This gave many players opportunities that they may not have had otherwise. One of these players was Pete Gray. The St. Louis Browns bought his semi-pro contract for a hefty $20,000. The sum raised eyebrows from Gray's new teammates, who didn't treat him with the fondest regard.

The consensus from the Browns players was that Gray was there as an attraction - a sideshow to bring in ticket sales. Gray didn't argue with words, deciding to let his performance on the diamond do the talking for him. He received national attention for his four-hit day in a doubleheader against the New York Yankees. Unfortunately, the media sensation surrounding Gray only furthered his teammates' beliefs that he was an attraction and not a true ballplayer.

This was something that weighed on Gray even after his baseball days were over. Did he really have baseball talent? Or, was it all true? That he only achieved his goal because he was a gate attraction?

No matter the reason behind his signing to the St. Louis Browns, Gray had made an unlikely dream a reality. With amputee soldiers returning from the war, the one-armed baseball player became a motivator to servicemen trying to understand how to live with their injuries.

Gray's career in the big leagues didn't last long. With the war ending and known baseball names returning home, Gray's days were numbered. He was also struggling at the plate when pitchers realized his one-armed batting method couldn't adjust to hit curveballs.

Gray will always be known as "The One-Armed Wonder" of baseball, as newspapers titled him during his career. However, like Jim Abbott, he was much more than his disability. Pete Gray pursued a dream that everyone else told him was impossible. He was a semi-pro MVP, hit home runs with one arm, and reached the big leagues. Most importantly, he inspired servicemen coming home battered and uncertain about their futures.

Did You Know?

- After baseball, Gray kept out of the public eye, even after stories renewed interest in him.

- In 1986, ABC aired a TV film called *A Winner Never Quits* based on Pete Gray's story.

- The unique glove that Gray used in his career is in the National Baseball Hall of Fame Museum in Cooperstown, New York

- Another effect of World War II draining talent from Major League Baseball was the introduction of the All-American Girls Professional Ball League, a women-only baseball league.

- Gray tried to enlist in the Army after the Japanese bombed Pearl Harbor. He was turned away because of his amputated arm. His response was, "If I could teach myself how to play baseball with one arm, I sure as hell could handle a rifle."

- In another show of patriotism, Gray turned down the Philadelphia Sports Writers recognizing him as the year's Most Courageous Athlete. "I can't fight, and so there is no courage about me. Courage belongs on the battlefield, not on the baseball diamond."

CHAPTER 13:

THE 2016 CHICAGO CUBS END A CENTURY-LONG WORLD SERIES DROUGHT

What do a goat, a black cat, Gatorade, and a man named Steve Bartman have in common? They are all pieces of an alleged curse that kept the Chicago Cubs from winning a World Series for over 100 years, between 1908 and 2016. They also failed to even *make it* to the World Series for over 75 years.

The 2016 World Series is a thrilling story in its own right, deserving of an entire chapter. But, setting the scene by addressing the goat in the room is important before telling that story.

Curses and superstitions in sports have been around for ages. Baseball is no exception; it may even be extreme. Baseball has seen its fair share of curses - Curse of the Bambino, of Coogan's Bluff, of Rocky Colavito, and, in the Cubs' case, the Curse of the Billy Goat. Every curse has the same general story: a team hasn't won the World Series in too many years, so there must be a hex, curse, spell, or some bad juju at play.

The longer a team remains winless, the more real the curse becomes. So, when you're the Chicago Cubs, with over 100 years of winless seasons, the Curse of the Billy Goat started to become a bonafide jinx to fans.

As a sports curse transforms from a made-up hoodoo to reality in fans' eyes, every failure becomes further evidence. When the cursed team makes a bad trade, a top player has a season-ending injury, or the team loses in the playoffs, it conjures conversations about the curse.

The Chicago Cubs, over their century-long drought, had many instances that seemed too bizarre *not* to be manifestations of a bewitchment.

Beginning and Middle of the Curse

The origin and namesake of the Chicago Cubs' curse is thanks to Billy Sianis. It was Game 4 of the 1945 World Series between the Detroit Tigers and the soon-to-be-cursed Chicago Cubs. Sianis was the owner of a nearby bar named the Billy Goat Tavern. The Chicago resident's love for goats went beyond just naming his business after the animal. He actually owned one as a pet.

Sianis' love for Murphy, his pet goat, drove the tavern owner to want to enjoy Game 4 of the 1945 World Series with his horned friend. Unfortunately, ticket booth attendees at Wrigley Field weren't keen on Sianis' request for two tickets, one for him and one for Murphy. In other accounts of the story, Sianis and Murphy actually made it through the gate and to their seats. However, other spectators didn't enjoy sitting next to the goat. Thus, Wrigley Field staff asked the pair to leave.

In either case, Mr. Sianis was not pleased. What transpired next also shifts slightly depending on the account. (Origin stories for curses always tend to be foggy on the exact details). The most common version of the story is Sianis declaring to the Wrigley staff, "Them Cubs, they ain't gonna win no more." Another version says Sianis sent a letter to Mr. Wrigley himself, but the sentiments of the telegraph are the same.

It's hard to take a man seriously when he's trying to watch a baseball game with his goat. That said, his words started to sink in by the end of the World Series. The Cubs, leading the series 2-1 entering Game 4, fell behind four runs and never came back. They'd lose Game 5 and win Game 6 to force a decisive final match. The Detroit Tigers smashed five runs in the first inning of Game 7, and that was it. They were World Series Champions by the end of the afternoon and the Chicago Cubs, true to Sianis' words, didn't win.

Sianis and Murphy aside, talk of curses in Chicago didn't start gaining traction for another 24 years. Enter the black cat. The 1969 Cubs seemed on a collision course with the playoffs. They held a solid first-place lead for the NL Pennant over most of the season. Plus, their lineup was juiced with several future Hall of Famers, including Ernie Banks, Ron Santo, Billy Williams, and Ferguson Jenkins.

In the home stretch of the regular season, the New York Mets started closing the gap in the standings. The two teams met on September 9 when an interesting event occurred. Ron Santo was waiting to bat when a black cat found its way onto the field of Shea Stadium. It walked right by Santo, drawing a thunderous roar of approval from the home crowd of the Mets. The cat circled Santo and stopped near the top of the visiting Cubs' dugout for a moment. After a brief staring contest with the Cubs' bench, the cat exited stage left.

It was an eerie symbol that marked what was yet to come. The Cubs lost the game and several more. Meanwhile, the Mets hit a 10-game win streak and slingshot past Chicago, knocking them out of the race for good.

The 1984 season was another year where everything seemed to line up for the Chicago Cubs. They had mega talent in Ryne Sandberg, a solid pitching staff, and other critical pieces. They even tried to make amends with the curse by bringing a goat onto the field during Opening Day ceremonies. It seemed to work. The Cubs were on a trajectory for the World Series, winning an NL-best 96 games and battling to the best-of-five NLCS against the San Diego Padres.

Again, talk of curses appeared. In the must-win Game 5, a ball skipped through the legs of first baseman Leo Durham. It opened the door for San Diego to tie the game and eventually score additional runs. It was another disastrous end for the Cubs. Allegedly, Durham's glove was sticky from spilled Gatorade in the dugout, which accounted for the fielding error. It made no difference that the error only allowed the tying run and not the three after it. It also didn't matter that Durham had made several successful plays already. Once you're cursed, anything can be another source of it, even spilled Gatorade.

The final chapter of the Chicago Cubs curse is one of the saddest. Steve Bartman was a lifelong Cubs fan, lucky enough to grab front-row tickets along the left field foul line to Game 6 of the 2003 NLCS. The game featured the Florida Marlins and the Cubs. Chicago needed just five more outs to reach the World Series.

Marlins player Luis Castillo popped up along the foul line, just in front of Bartman's seat. Moises Alou came to make the catch, leaping up to the top of the wall. Bartman and other fans made a play on the ball first, deflecting it out of reach of Alou. Kept alive by the interference, Castillo drew a walk. The Marlins came to life and scored eight runs to force Game 7.

Bartman became the most hated man in Chicago overnight. Immediately following the play, fans in Bartman's section shouted obscenities and threw debris at him. One individual came and poured a beer directly on his head. The outrage was so bad he needed a police escort to leave the stadium. The abuse didn't stop. People issued death threats and began showing up at his house.

Even after the initial hatred stopped, Bartman remained a pariah in the Chicago area. It would take the Cubs winning the World Series for the city to finally forgive him.

The 2016 World Series

The length of the Cubs' World Series drought is something only a few teams could touch. Most teams haven't been around even half that time. The Red Sox are the first team to come to mind with an 86-year (also cursed) World Series - that they ended in 2004. The Cleveland Guardians are another older team that hasn't tasted the Commissioner's Trophy in decades. They haven't won since 1948.

Interestingly, when the Chicago Cubs won their title in 2016, it was against the Guardians. Entering the World Series, the two teams combined for 176 seasons without championship honors. The underdog story made the 2016 series notable, but how the games unfolded made it one of the best of all time.

Game 1 took place in Cleveland. Kenny Lofton, a long-time hero for the Guardians, threw out the first pitch. The home-field advantage proved useful. Cleveland scored two runs in the first inning, one in the fourth, and three in the eighth. Meanwhile, Corey Kluber's pitching was lights out against Chicago. The final score was 6-0 Cleveland.

144

The next game was a 180-degree turn. This time, Chicago's pitching, led by Jake Arrieta, kept Cleveland's batters fooled. The Cubs scattered some runs and had a three-run rally in the fifth inning to come out on top 5-1.

With the series tied 1-1, it was time for Chicago to return home to Wrigley Field. Surely, with home-field advantage, they could put away a few games and gain an edge over Cleveland! The fanfare before the game included Billy Williams throwing out the first pitch and actor Bill Murray enthusiastically singing "Take Me Out to the Ball Game" in the seventh inning. Game 3 ended with a 1-0 score. Four Cleveland pitchers combined to shut out the Cubs' batters.

The second game at Wrigley Field (Game 4) wasn't so close. Chicago got out to a one-run lead against Corey Kluber in the first inning, but Cleveland scored seven unanswered runs afterwards. Dexter Fowler hit a home run for Chicago in the eighth, but it wasn't enough to overcome the deficit. The Cleveland Guardians needed just one more win to, once again, send the Cubs home without a World Series title.

With every game becoming a must-win affair, the Chicago Cubs began to dig their heels in against the Guardians. They struck for three runs in the fourth inning, knocking Trevor Bauer, the Cleveland starter, out of the game. It ended up being the only run support the Cubbies needed. The high-velocity closer, Aroldis Chapman came in to deliver eight outs of support and finish the game.

Game 6 brought the series back to Progressive Field in Cleveland. The Cubs would need to win the next two games as visitors to secure the World Series title. They got off to a great start, scoring three runs in the first inning during a two-out rally. In the fourth inning, the Cubs struck big again. Addison Russel launched a grand slam to tack four more runs on the board. Cleveland had a few one-run innings but never came back, losing the game 9-3.

Game 7

There have been a few times in World Series history that a team came back from a 3-1 deficit. The Chicago Cubs, hoping to be the next on the list, went with their ace, Kyle Hendricks, to start the game. Cleveland's starter, Corey Kluber, had already given the Cubs issues in Game 1 and Game 4.

Kluber didn't seem to faze Dexter Fowler, who hit a lead-off home run, the first player to ever do so in a Game 7 World Series situation. However, Cleveland answered back in the third inning. The rest of the game went much like this, with one team scoring and the other answering back.

The Cubs put up two runs in the top of the fourth inning on a sacrifice fly and double. Then, another two runs in the fifth inning. Javier Baez hit a first-pitch home run, knocking Kluber out of the game. Andrew Miller came into relief and promptly gave up another run on a walk and RBI single. The score was 5-1, but Cleveland replied promptly.

In the bottom of the fifth inning, Joe Maddon, the Cubs manager, pulled Hendricks after he walked a batter. Jon Lester came into the game with his catcher, David Ross. A Ross throwing error and a Lester wild pitch combined to allow two runs to be scored, closing Chicago's lead to 5-3.

Ross made up for the error in the sixth inning with a solo home run, pushing the lead to three runs. But, by the end of the eighth inning, Cubs fans everywhere had a baseball-sized lump in their throat. Even though Lester put away the first two batters, Maddon again went to the bench, bringing Aroldis Chapman into the game, despite his workload over the past few days.

Chapman nicknamed the Cuban Missile, didn't have his typical, explosive pitching. He gave up a double out of the gate that scored a run. The next batter, Rajai Davis, hit a two-run home run to tie the game. It felt like an absolute blunder, starting with Maddon bringing in Chapman on little rest. But there was still more baseball left.

The Cubs had opportunities to score in the ninth inning. They scattered several base runners before Francisco Lindor on the Guardians made a spectacular play to grab the last out and prevent a possible run or two from scoring.

Luckily, Chapman found his groove in the bottom of the ninth and retired the side.

Then it began to rain. There was a 17-minute delay before play could resume due to the weather. During this time, the Cubs called a meeting inside the clubhouse next to the dugout. Jason Heyward led the meeting and used the delay time to rally the troops. With renewed spirits and clearer weather, the Chicago Cubs came up to bat and began producing runs.

Kyle Schwarber got the Cubs' offense going with a single and was replaced by a pinch-runner. A deep fly ball by Kris Bryant moved the runner to second base. The next batter was walked intentionally, bringing up Ben Zobrist with runners on first and second. He smoked a ball down the left field line and into the corner, more than enough to score the runner on second. But Chicago wasn't done scoring.

Cleveland issued another intentional walk, this time to the red-hot Addison Russel, hoping to get to Miguel Montero. Montero was batting a measly .091 in the postseason. He picked a good time to start turning his plate performance around, hitting a single into left field and scoring another run. The Guardians would turn to Trevor Bauer and eventually get out of the inning, but the damage was done: 8-6.

Carl Edwards Jr. got the ball in the bottom of the 10th, needing just three outs to secure the first Cubs World Series in over 100 years. He recorded the first two swiftly, but the last one was a challenge. After walking Brandon Guyer, Rajai Davis, still high off his eighth-inning home run, struck again. He hit an RBI single into center. There was just one run separating the two teams.

Chicago made yet another pitching change, bringing in Mike Montgomery. Despite never having a save in his career, the pitcher did exactly what he needed to in this late-inning relief position. He got Michael Martinez to hit a soft grounder to third. Kris Bryant came charging in to field the ball and threw it to Anthony Rizzo for the final out at first.

Afterwards, Rizzo called the rain delay "the most important thing to happen to the Chicago Cubs in the past 100 years." He claimed it gave them the late-game push to win and shifted the momentum back to Chicago's favor. "I don't think there's any way we win the game without it."

Turns out, the best cure for a billy goat curse is some rainwater.

Did You Know?

- The Cleveland Guardians are still looking for their first World Series title since 1948, a drought of 74 years, the longest in baseball.

- David Ross, the backup catcher for the Cubs during their historic 2016 championship title, became the team's manager three years later. Despite his backup role, many teammates said Ross' veteran experience and clubhouse influence were vital parts of their season and World Series title.

- Theo Epstein was the GM for the Red Sox in 2004 when they ended their 86-year World Series drought. He was also the President of Baseball Operations for the 2016 Chicago Cubs.

- Terry Francona, Cleveland's manager, was also the manager for the 2004 World Series Boston Red Sox team.

- Game 7 of the 2016 World Series was the first extra-inning Game 7 since 1997 when the Florida Marlins defeated the Cleveland Guardians 3-2 over 11 innings.

- The Cleveland Guardians have their own curse to explain the 74-year World Series drought. It is the Curse of Rocky Colavito. The owner of the Cleveland team traded Colavito in 1960 after he led the American League in home runs. It outraged fans and apparently, continues to do so.

CHAPTER 14:

THE 2004 BOSTON RED SOX BREAK THE CURSE OF THE BAMBINO

Chicago's billy goat drama isn't even baseball's most notorious curse. That prestige has to be given to the Curse of the Bambino and the Boston Red Sox. The origin story for this baseball hex involves the trading of Babe Ruth to the New York Yankees in 1918. Boston won the World Series that year, with Ruth. After trading him to the Yankees, they didn't win a single one. The Yankees, meanwhile, accumulated 27 Championships, five of them with Ruth.

It wasn't just the lack of World Series titles that led Red Sox Nation to believe in the Curse of the Bambino so vehemently. It was the gruesome way they would *lose* opportunities to win the championship each year.

The Babe-less Red Sox wouldn't reach the World Series until 1946. Against the Cardinals in Game 7, Boston's shortstop, Johnny Pesky, made what many fans claim was a mental error. After receiving the cut-off throw, he didn't immediately throw home to stop the charging Enos Slaughter from scoring. He held the ball for valuable seconds that allowed the Cardinals to score a decisive run. An injured and ineffective Ted Williams was another reason Sox fans felt the team's World Series hopes were doomed in 1946.

Over 20 years later, they reached the World Series again (and again faced the Cardinals), only for manager Dick Williams to jinx the team before Game 7. When a reporter asked Williams which Boston pitcher would start the final game, he replied, "Lonborg and champagne," referencing the Red Sox ace Jim Lonborg and that the team would enjoy champagne after winning the title. Whether it truly jinxed the team or not, his comments angered the Cardinals players, meaning they came into the game with a chip on their shoulders.

In 1975, the Red Sox lost a lead in the ninth inning of Game 7. A few years later, the Red Sox were knocked out of the World Series again. This time it was a Bucky Dent home run that kissed the top of the wall before exiting the field. If the ball was even a fraction of an inch lower (or the wall a fraction of an inch taller) the ball stays in the field and keeps the Red Sox World Series dreams alive.

The 1986 World Series was the most calamitous defeat yet. The Red Sox had the New York Mets on the ropes in Game 6. Leading the series 3-2, they only needed to win one more game. Boston went up one run in the 10th inning, the Mets had only three outs left. Then, the Curse of the Bambino unraveled Boston's hopes entirely.

Red Sox pitcher Bob Stanley threw a wild pitch to score a tying run. Boston needed to get out of the inning without any more damage if they wanted to clinch the World Series in Game 6. The inning should have been over when Mookie Wilson hit a routine ground ball to first base. The play was routine for Bill Buckner at first. He was a great defensive player. Unfortunately, fate had other ideas. The ball squeaked between his legs, allowing the winning run to score.

The Red Sox lost Game 7 two days later. The collapse of the 1986 Red Sox influenced writer George Vecsey to make official what many Red Sox fans already felt. The team was cursed. Worse yet, the Bambino's Curse still had one more devastating song to play.

Overcoming Another Tragedy

This story does have a happy ending. The Red Sox would win the World Series in 2004. However, they still had one more unfortunate event to overcome: the 2003 American League Championship Series against their bitter rivals, the New York Yankees. The series went the extra mile, reaching the 11th frame of Game 7.

The Red Sox actually had a decent lead in the eighth inning, ahead by three runs. In a questionable managerial decision, the team's skipper left starter Pedro Martinez in the game. Martinez had already put two base runners on, and his pitch count was over 100.

When manager Grady Little visited the mound, it seemed obvious to everyone there would be a pitch change. Martinez protested, promising Little he still had something. The manager conceded and left the starter in the game. The

Yankees jumped on the tired pitcher and notched three runs to tie the game.

The Yankees brought in the ineffable Mariano Rivera, who pitched three scoreless innings, pushing the game to the 11th and final inning. On the first pitch of the bottom of the 11th, Aaron Boone hit a walk-off home run to send the Yankees to the World Series. For Red Sox Nation, it was history repeating itself all over again.

In the following season, the Red Sox and Yankees met again in the ALCS. It was an opportunity for Boston to redeem itself against the Bronx Bombers. They didn't make it easy on themselves, losing the first three games of the seven-game series. No team in history had ever come back from an 0-3 deficit in the playoffs. The Red Sox were about to become the first, and they were about to do it against none other than the New York Yankees, the team at the heart of their curse and responsible for so many of its chapters.

The 2004 ALCS, Down 0-3

The 2004 Yankees team had not lost four games in a row to a team all year. They hadn't had a losing streak longer than three games since mid-April. Now, the Red Sox were facing the team in their dominant postseason form. This was when the Yankees thrived, and, historically, Boston did not. Worse for the Red Sox, they were entering Game 4 after a crushing 9-18 defeat the night before.

With the odds heavily against Boston, many fans had already accepted the most likely outcome - the Red Sox would end the season with another disappointing loss to the Yankees in the playoffs. The best they could hope for was to win at least one game and avoid the embarrassment of being swept by the rivals. Yet, there was still that twinge of hope left. The season wasn't over. There was still time, no matter how unlikely or implausible the desired outcome was. Possibility is a powerful motivator.

Through the first four innings of Game 4, everything seemed to point to another Yankees win. Alex Rodriguez had put New York ahead with a home run in the third. Meanwhile, the Red Sox hitters couldn't put anything together against Yankees pitcher Orlando Hernández. They had just one hit through the first four innings.

Luckily, Boston's scoring drought ended in the fifth inning. Hernández pitched himself into a tough situation that led to a two-out rally. The Red Sox rally started with an RBI single from Orlando Cabrera. Then, David Ortiz hit the ball into centerfield to score two more runs and put his team up 3-2.

Momentum didn't stay on Boston's side for long. In the top of the sixth inning, the Red Sox infield misplayed several balls, allowing three Yankees to reach base on weak infield hits. The door was wide open for New York to retake the lead. For Boston fans, it felt like another chapter in their cursed history.

When the inning eventually ended, the score was 4-2 in favor of New York. It was a small relief that the Yankees only led by a small margin after the disastrous half-inning by Boston's defense. But time was quickly running out for the Red Sox to keep their season and World Series hopes alive.

It soon became the ninth inning. The 2004 Red Sox were down to their last three outs to make something happen. As expected, the Yankees handed the ball to Mariano Rivera, the team's masterful closer. Rivera was a hitter's worst nightmare during the regular season, but his playoff dominance, unbelievably, was at an even higher level.

Most of Rivera's appearances went his way, but this night in October did not. Boston's first batter, Kevin Millar, drew a walk. Immediately, Dave Roberts came into the game to pinch run. The next few moments became one of the rare pitcher-runner duels in baseball.

The Yankee closer threw over to first again and again and held the ball for as long as he could - anything to disrupt Roberts' timing. It was clear Roberts intended to steal. The Red Sox needed to get a runner into scoring position. When Rivera finally unleashed a pitch to home plate, the speedy Red Sox runner took off. He got the great jump he needed to reach second with everyone anticipating the theft. He slid in safely just before Derek Jeter's tag.

The Dave Roberts steal brought the Red Sox fans to life. The risky swiped bag proved to be the winning strategy. Bill Mueller would put enough charge into a ball to get it through the infield, allowing the speedy Roberts to wheel around third and score safely at home. The inning ended with a tied game.

Boston would seize Game 4 in the 12th inning. David Ortiz hit a walk-off, two-run home run that brought the home crowd at Fenway Park to their feet. There was still some fight left in Boston.

Another Long Night, Down 1-3

Game 4's extra-inning saga left players on both teams with little time to recover before the next game. They'd need the nerves and playoff baseball adrenaline to make up for this lack of rest. It didn't take long for the action to get started. The Red Sox put two runs up thanks to an Ortiz RBI single and a walk to Jason Varitek with the bases loaded. The Yankees answered with a solo home run, but little else for most of the game.

Missing some scattered scoring chances, the score remained 2-1 until the sixth inning. Red Sox ace Pedro Martínez, in what may have been his last game in a Red Sox uniform, faced little trouble thus far. But the Yankees batters began to find opportunities. Ruben Sierra and Jorge Posada reached base on hits before Martínez hit a batter to load the bases.

If Game 5 was a boxing fight card, the matchup that was about to happen would have undoubtedly been the headliner. Derek Jeter came to bat with the bases loaded against Martínez. Jeter was behind so many game-defining playoff moments that the media often took to calling him "Captain Clutch." He did his nickname justice by hitting a double down the first base line and catapulting the Yankees to another 4-2 lead.

Once more, the Red Sox had only a handful of chances left to mount a comeback and pull ahead. First, Ortiz, having already scored once in the game, would lift a solo home run to close the scoring gap to only one run. With the score sitting a 4-3, the game suddenly felt like a television show rerun. Kevin Millar walks; Dave Roberts pinch runs for Millar; a few batters later, Roberts touches home and ties the game.

The game entered extra innings, stretching to the 14th inning. Both teams were exhausted and deep into their bench and bullpens. When Ortiz came to bat, the scattered Red Sox fans at Yankee Stadium got to their feet. Not only was he the hero of Game 4, less than 24 hours ago, but he'd already scored twice this game. It was the exact person Red Sox Nation wanted at the bat. And he didn't disappoint!

Ortiz hit a line-drive single to score the winning run and put the almost-six-hour game to bed.

The Bloody Sock

Two weeks before Game 6, on October 5, Curt Schilling was pitching in another meaningful game. It was Game 1 of the ALDS series between Boston and the Los Angeles Angels. During this game, Schilling tore a tendon sheath in his ankle. Every step became painful, and Schilling questioned his ability to pitch at all.

His first appearance against the Yankees in Game 1 suggested that the injured ankle negatively impacted his control and power on the mound. The Yankees jumped on him quickly and often in Game 1. A week later, the Red Sox turned the ball over to him once more, hoping the extra week of healing made the difference.

Before the game, Schilling underwent minor surgery in the training room. The team doctor hoped the procedure would provide a temporary fix, giving the pitcher enough relief to pitch through one of the biggest games of his life. Fresh from this surgical patch job, Schilling lumbered out to the mound and began throwing. Camera crews immediately began to highlight the red stain on the pitcher's sock.

Schilling's bloody sock became the central topic at hand. Every broadcaster and network kept discussing the blood spot. Was it getting larger? Was it real? And, the most important question for the Red Sox, could he pitch?

Behind all the obsessing over the bloody sock, Schilling had settled into a groove and pitched successfully through seven innings. On an injured ankle, he allowed only one run. Meanwhile, the Red Sox had put four on the board.

After his exit, Boston reliever Bronson Arroyo gave up an RBI single to Derek Jeter. Beyond this small stumble, the score would remain 4-2. The injured Schilling and his bloody sock got the win.

History Made

The Red Sox had won three games in a row and pushed the 2004 ALCS to a final showdown in Game 7. With the momentum clearly in Boston's favor, Red Sox fans were trying to contain their excitement. There were still a lot of apprehensions. After all, this was the Red Sox. It was only a matter of time before they would let you down. Perhaps the comeback was just setting Red Sox Nation up for a crueler and more heartbreaking downfall. "I know how this ends because I've been watching it all my life," said one Sox fan prior to Game 7.

With everything on the line, Game 7 was lackluster compared to the previous three. There was no late-inning heroics by David Ortiz (although he would get the Red Sox on the scoreboard first with a two-run home run). No Dave Roberts stealing a base to get into a scoring position. And there was certainly no bloody sock. Johnny Damon cracked the game open with a grand slam home run to make it 6-0. After a few more innings, he'd hit another home, making the score 8-1.

That was more than enough run support for the Red Sox. Starter Derek Lowe kept the Yankees hitters at bay with just one hit over six innings. By the end of the game, the Yankees would score just three runs, giving the Boston Red Sox the pass to the World Series.

They hadn't won the World Series yet, but it didn't matter. This was almost better. It was justice for the 2003 ALCS, Bucky Dent, and 86 years of cursed torment. Overcoming the 0-3 deficit against the Yankees was the event necessary to remedy Boston baseball once and for all.

Seven days later, they would win Game 4 and complete a sweep of the Cardinals to win the World Series. Since claiming the title in 2004, the Boston Red Sox have won three more times (2007, 2013, and 2018)

Did You Know?

- Yankees closer Mariano Rivera gets a lot of credit for his postseason track record. However, in the 2004 playoffs, Boston's Keith Foulke was the more dominant reliever. He allowed just one earned run over the entire postseason. Many of his save opportunities lasted multiple innings, too.

- The 2004 Red Sox team is fondly remembered as "the idiots." The nickname captured their carefree, fun demeanor. "We try to eliminate the thinking," explained Johnny Damon, often credited for originating the nickname. "We've tried to let our natural abilities take over. If we use our brains, we're only hurting the team."

- Stephen King and Stewart O'Nan wrote *Faithful*, chronicling the 2004 Boston Red Sox team. It was pure luck (and perhaps faith) that their book happened to chronicle *the* season.

- Curt Schilling was a new addition to the Red Sox in 2004, acquired in a trade with his previous club, the Arizona Diamondbacks. Prior to the season, Ford Motor Company ran commercials featuring Schilling hitchhiking in the Arizona desert. When a driver stops, the pitcher says he's headed to Boston to break an 86-year-old curse.

- The 2005 movie *Fever Pitch* depicts a couple falling into, out of, and then back into love with one another around the events of the 2004 Red Sox season. The movie's original plot had the Red Sox losing in the playoffs. When Boston completed their comeback against the Yankees and won the World Series versus the Cardinals, the ending had to be rewritten and certain scenes filmed again.

- Several members of the 2004 Red Sox team were also present for the Chicago Cubs ending their drought in 2016.

CHAPTER 15:

MIKE PIAZZA HITS THE MOST SIGNIFICANT HOME RUN IN AMERICAN HISTORY

Sports have a puppet string effect on human emotions. You can feel joy, anger, sadness, nervousness, excitement, grief, sorrow, relief, and more. Sometimes, fans rifle through *all* these feelings in just a single game.

In the same respect, sports can provide a necessary break from the lows of life. A bad day can feel a little bit better when the home team wins. This is what pushed FDR to officially request that baseball leagues continue during World War II. He sent an open letter to the league presidents at the time that read:

> "What I am going to say is solely a personal and not an official point of view. I honestly feel that it would be best for the country to keep baseball going. There will be fewer people unemployed and everybody will work longer hours and harder than ever before. And that means that they ought to have **a chance for recreation and for taking their minds off their work** even more than before...."

Baseball provides a sometimes-necessary distraction, especially during difficult times. This is ingrained into the soul of baseball. Fans today often question the 162-game length of the season. It's a lot - teams play nearly every day. There's little time off, which leads to fatigue and a higher risk of injury.

The lengthy schedule was designed strategically to benefit the American people. It provided a source of leisure and entertainment to combat long, arduous workdays. Stretching the schedule as much as possible, starting in early Spring and ending in the middle of Fall, ensured Americans had baseball as a pleasant distraction for as long as possible.

At no time in history did America need more of a distraction than in the aftermath of the September 11 terrorist attacks. Mike Piazza and the New York Mets played a home game against the Atlanta Braves, the first game held in the city since the attacks. It would become one of the most important games in baseball history, not because of standings or who was playing, but because of its positive impact on the spirit of New York City and the American people.

An Unlikely Star

Any player drafted by a Major League Baseball team is one step closer to achieving their goal of playing in the big leagues. However, the MLB draft is long. In 1988, the year the Los Angeles Dodgers would draft Mike Piazza, it consisted of 62 rounds, meaning 1,390 players would be selected. In comparison, the NFL and NFL drafts are only seven rounds long. The NBA finishes its draft in just two rounds.

With such a huge pool of drafted players, the odds of making it to the professional level are slim. Most players spend the majority of their careers trying to develop their skills in the minor leagues. They may scatter a few MLB appearances but never experience being an everyday starter for a team at this level.

Teams draft players based on several factors. Early-round draft picks are guys expected to become future pros. Meanwhile, late draft picks are seen as project players. There are few expectations that these athletes will develop the skills necessary to play at the MLB level. Sometimes, late draft picks surprise everyone. There may be a scout eager to take credit and boasting that they 'knew all along,' but the truth is the odds of a fringe player making it to the MLB are infinitesimal.

So, it may come as a surprise to know that future Hall of Famer and legendary Mets catcher Mike Piazza was not, as one might expect, drafted early. In fact, he was the very last player selected in the 1988 draft, taken as the 1,390th pick in the final round. The decision to draft Piazza wasn't even a baseball one. Tommy Lasorda in the Dodgers organization chose him as a favor to Piazza's father.

At the time, Piazza was a first baseman for Miami-Dade Community College. This sheds some light on his unknown status entering the 1988 draft. MLB scouts tend to focus on bigger schools and rarely, if ever, attend community college games. Thus, his talents went under the radar.

Nonetheless, Lasorda was skeptical of Piazza's abilities. To give him the best chances, he encouraged the young player to shift positions to catcher. Lasorda even arranged for Piazza to attend an intensive training camp in the Dominican Republic to help him learn his new role. At this position, he'd have better odds of making it to the big leagues. Many catchers earn an MLB roster spot as a backup catcher in the bullpen, having the job of warming up pitchers before they enter the game.

Piazza's skills, particularly with a bat, quickly became apparent to the Dodgers club. He had also learned how to play his new position at a high level. In 1992, just four short years after being drafted last, he made his Major League Baseball debut in early September. With the season almost over, Piazza only played in 21 games. He batted .232.

The 1993 season put Piazza's name into the vernacular of every baseball-tuned mind in the country. Not only did he get the nod to play in the All-Star Game but he also won the National League Rookie of the Year Award. Batting an impressive .318 during the season, Piazza hit 35 home runs and batted his teammates in 112 times. It was a landmark season and the first of many for the rookie.

Over the next decade, Piazza would return to the All-Star Game each year. He nearly made MVP honors in back-to-back years, finishing second in the voting, first behind Ken Caminiti and then Larry Walker. The 1997 season was arguably his best ever. He batted .362 and hit 40 home runs and 124 RBIs.

Prior to the 1998 season, the Los Angeles Dodgers traded Piazza (along with Todd Zeile) to the Florida Marlins, acquiring Gary Sheffield, Bobby Bonilla, and other players in return. Most baseball fans don't remember Piazza's time with the Marlins because it wasn't very long. He was traded a second time just a week later to the Mets. He played only five games with the Marlins.

September 11, 2001

Mike Piazza did what he was known for in his season with the Mets. He batted .348 with his new team, clubbing 23 home runs and attended his sixth All-Star Game in a row. The next two years were some of his best with the New York ball club. In '99 he hit 40 home runs and maintained a .303 average. A year later, he hit two fewer home runs but pushed his average to .324 for the season.

He quickly became beloved by Mets fans, particularly in the 2000 season. His performance at and behind the plate helped the team reach the World Series for the first time since the Miracle Mets of 1986.

171

The love for Mike Piazza exploded dramatically late in the 2001 season. New York was trying to heal from the single most devastating event to take place on its soil. It's an event that needs no explanation. But, to properly understand the impact of Piazza's role in uplifting the spirit of New York and America, it's important to relive the traumatic events of September 11, 2001.

On this morning, which will forever live in infamy in the hearts and minds of the American people, 19 hijackers took control of four commercial flights in a calculated plan to inflict devastation. The terrorists crashed two planes into the World Trade Center in New York City. A third plane hit the Pentagon in Arlington, Virginia. Thanks to the efforts of courageous passengers, the fourth plane was diverted from its intended target in Washington D.C. and crashed into a field in Pennsylvania.

The attacks claimed the lives of nearly 3,000 people. The lives unfairly claimed by the nefarious efforts of the terrorists almost become a footnote compared to the effect it had on the country. September 11 shattered the American people's sense of security. Nothing felt safe or "normal" anymore. It put a gaping hole in the heart of the American spirit in a way that felt impossible to repair.

In response to the attacks, life came to a sudden stop in the US. Bud Selig, the acting baseball commissioner, declared Major League Baseball would pause playing until the following week. This would give time for players to spend time with families, for America to focus on the tragedies at hand, and for security at ballparks to be heightened.

During this break, players did their best to uplift their communities. In New York City, the place most affected by the attacks, this felt like an impossible task. What could a baseball player do at a time like this?

The Home Run That Healed

Ten days after the terrorist attacks on the 11th, the New York Mets hosted the Atlanta Braves at home. It was the first major sporting event in the city since the attacks. With no sense of safety or security left, there was a significant fear that such a large crowd in New York City could be a target for another attack.

Ignoring these dreadful feelings, fans and players arrived at Shea Stadium. The ballpark was adorned in the red, white, and blue of the American flag, and the Mets players opted to wear hats representing the fire and police departments of New York, instead of their typical uniform attire.

Initially, the players were warned against this because it could make them targets if there was another attack during the game. Piazza and his teams ignored the concerns. It was what they needed to do to show their appreciation for the people that had spent tireless hours in the last 10 days repairing the city and saving New Yorker lives.

Despite all of the patriotic fanfare, there was still a thick feeling of pain and uneasiness in the crowd. For the first few innings, fans did their best to enjoy a baseball game. Yet, the whirlwind of emotions caused by the attacks was still ever-present in their minds. These emotions started to shift late in the game.

By the bottom of the eighth inning, the score was 2-1 in favor of the visiting Atlanta team. When Braves pitcher (and a New York native) Steve Karsay walked Edgardo Alfonzo to bring Piazza up to bat, the entirety of Shea Stadium came alive. Fans began chanting "Let's go, Mets!" For most in attendance, it was the first time they had something to cheer for since the terrorist attacks rocked the city less than two weeks prior.

Piazza took the first pitch for a strike. He rarely ever swung at the first pitch. Karsay's next pitch was intended to be off the outside of the plate to get Piazza to chase. Instead, it was right over the middle of the plate. The sound of the ball off the bat brought the New York crowd to its feet. They knew it was gone before it left the stadium, disappearing into the camera tower in left field.

There were 41,000 people in attendance that night, mostly first responders or family members of the victims of the attacks. They were people who had been at the heart of the destruction both physically and emotionally. They were people who, for the last 10 days, had felt nothing but pain, confusion, and loss. They were people who had not felt normal since the early hours of September 11, before their entire worlds were changed.

With that one home run, Mike Piazza gave all those people something to cheer for. It may have been just a brief moment of jubilation, but it had a significant impact on the restoration of the New York and American spirit. It was a home run that healed a city in one of the rare moments in sports that is much bigger than the game itself.

Did You Know?

- When Piazza was inducted into the Hall of Fame, he chose to be inducted as a Met.

- The uniform Piazza wore during the game rotates between the Hall of Fame, the September 11th Memorial Museum, and Citi Field.

- Piazza is one of only a handful of players to hit home runs in more than 40 stadiums.

- Because of new procedures for the MLB draft, Piazza will likely hold his spot as the lowest-drafted player to make the Hall of Fame for good.

- Ted Williams met a 16-year-old Piazza and, after talking to the player, gave him the stamp of approval. Williams told Piazza's father that his son could hit 25-30 home runs in the big leagues. Piazza relayed this to Tommy Lasorda, saying, "If Ted Williams put that handle on him, he's going to be a hitter."

- Piazza is considered one of the best-hitting catchers. He hit a record 396 home runs as a catcher. He's also fourth in runs among catchers and has more Silver Slugger awards than backstops.

CONCLUSION

Baseball remains America's treasured pastime. It's been the most persistent source of entertainment and athletic achievement in the history of the country, providing leisure and relief during times of crisis and tragedy.

At times, the sport has led the country in social change, reminding its citizens that things like equality and fair play should be afforded to everyone, inside baseball and out.

The game's Greats become more than just the athletes we cheer for. They become key characters in American drama. Their personas are larger than the home runs they hit and more carefully crafted than the pitches they threw.

There is no greater storytelling resource than baseball. These 15 examples, from Satchel Paige to Mike Piazza, are just drops in an ocean of folklore and memories that surround the game of baseball. A man can forget his own name, but he will still remember the day he saw Ted Williams hit a triple, or Mickey Mantle smash a screaming line drive.

Baseball is eternal. It is sport, business, tradition, life, and even religion. The rules are simple, but the history is as complex as the country it symbolizes.

Made in United States
North Haven, CT
21 December 2023

46467586R00104